OVERSIZE 747 VAN

Van Dooren, Adrienne.

The house that faux
built : transform your
c2007.

THE HOUSE THAT

Transform Your Home Using Paints, Plasters & Creativity

ADRIENNE VAN DOOREN

EAST
CAMBRIDGE
PRESS

THE HOUSE THAT FAUX BUILT

Copyright © 2007 by Adrienne van Dooren

First Edition-hardcover
Published by East Cambridge Press
249 North Larch Street, Anaheim, CA 92805
(571) 239-6656
www.eastcambridgepress.com
Distributed in the USA by Pathway Book Service:
pbs@pathwaybook.com

Photography: David Galen, Galen Photography
Specialty photographs by Omar Selinas, High Tech Photography
In progress photography provided by, Suzanne Leedy, Ceil Glembocki, Lisa Turner, Tania Seabock, Ashley Spencer, and Louise Kraft
Graphic Design: Adrienne van Dooren
Graphic Production: Vicky Nuttall
Editing: Lorre Lei Jackson and Patti Newton

Submit proposed changes or corrections to info@fauxhouse.com
Quantity Discounts are available- (see order form) For personalized/ corporate print runs call 571-239-6656

Publisher intends to update book regularly so that it serves as a living, growing resource. Those wishing to be included as a sponsor or resource should contact info@ fauxhouse.com. The purpose of this project and book is to support victims of natural disasters. Proceeds from this book will fund one or more homes for Habitat for Humanity - New Orleans. The proceeds from the birdhouse auction were donated to Noah's Wish for animal rescue. As of this printing we have raised over $45,000 of $75,000 is required to build one house and over $1,500 for animal rescue. Those who wish to contribute toward the house may do so through us or directly to Habitat for Humanity - New Orleans on line or by mail. Please notate the funds are for "The Habitat House that Faux Built."

Publishers Cataloging - In- Publication Data:

van Dooren, Adrienne.

The house that faux built: transform your home using paint, plaster & creativity / Adrienne van Dooren.--1st ed.--Anahem, CA : East Cambridge Press, 2007.

p.;cm

ISBN 13: 978-0-9778967-0-7
ISBN 10: 0-9778967-0-6

1. Interior decoration. 2. Art in Interior decoration 3. Dwellings-Remodeling. I. Title

NK1990 .V36 2007   2007923612
747--dc22   0708

Printed in the United States of America

Contents

Author's Note

I'm often asked how this project came about. It started as a thought; an idea that expanded into action as many artists shared the same vision. In the end the project exceeded all expectations, becoming the decorative artisan's version of "We are the World." Over a hundred top artists worked together in "concert" to fund a House to be built by Habitat for Humanity-New Orleans for Katrina victims, therefore we named the project the "*The House that Faux Built*." An international birdhouse painting contest was added to aid the animals made homeless by the hurricanes and to insure that any artist who wanted to participate in this project could do so.

Once funded, many of the artists and volunteers will go to New Orleans to work on the Habitat house. A portion of proceeds from the sale of this book will go to Habitat-New Orleans to continue this work, with the remainder reimbursing past costs of keeping the house unoccupied and helping to fund future projects.

It is also our hope that this book will increase public awareness of the incredible advances in faux and decorative painting since the sponging fad of the 90's and serve as a catalyst for ideas and further advancements in decorative painting.

Adrienne van Dooren

Acknowledgements

I'd like to thank the Academy....no seriously, Fauxcademy, for giving me the push to get this project started. It was there that I witnessed the incredible advancements in faux and demonstrations from some of the top faux artists in the country. My gratitude goes to Mark-Victor Hansen who spoke and encouraged us all to live our dreams. This project has allowed me to do just that.

But this project isn't about me–it is about the efforts and gifts of over a hundred artists, volunteers and sponsors who came together to support hurricane victims through art.

These artists, the top in their fields, not only gave of their time and talents on very short notice, but also bore all costs of travel and expenses. Some of these artists were the instructors/mentors who helped me transition from Army to Artist (e.g. .Nicola Vigini, Sean Crosby, Kelly King, Mary Kingslan-Gabilisco Sheri Hoeger, and Melanie Royals). Some (Joanne Nash, Wanda Timmons, Adrian Greenfield, Paulette Piazza, past classmates, and SALI members) were old friends. Others–Caroline Woldenberg, Amanda Sumerlin, Micheal Gross, Chesna Koch, Julie Miles, Brad Duerson, Tania Seabock, the Kershners, Ashley Spencer, Amy Ketteran, Deb Drager, Barth White, Susie Goldenberg, Donna Phelps, Donna Smith, Ron Layman, Maggie Oneill, Jacek Prowenski, Rose Wilde, Leonard Pardon, Dan Mahlmann, Gary Arvanitopulos, Gary Lord, and others) I'd not known but asked to join based on their reputation or specialty. Like soldiers in the trenches (yes it often felt like that), we all bonded by working toward a common goal. Indeed everyone involved in the project deserves special recognition but in the interest of our national forests each artist and room captain and volunteer is featured in other portions of the book.

I would, however, like to give a special note of thanks to Ann Bayer the co-chair, and her husband Carl who who made this project a near full-time endeavor. Also special thanks to Patti Irwin–sponsorship chair, and Celeste Stewart–operations chair. Had it not been for these four, the House that Faux Built would never be have come to fruition.

We could not have succeeded without some incredibly dedicated volunteers. Many volunteers gave over 150 hours (Carolyn Spencer, Linda O'Neill, Rebecca Hotop, Chris Jackson, Lisa Turner, Michael Gross, Ceil Glembocki , Tracie Weir, and Carol Patterson) and none complained of the mundane grunt work that is 90% of such an endeavor. Our designers, Nancy AtLee and Mau-Don Nygen spent countless hours to find just the right furniture and accessories to complement the artist's work. Valerie Burchett took over as webmaster at the last minute and did a super job!

Our deepest appreciation to all our sponsors who gave selflessly in support of this project, with a special note of thanks to Modello Designs™, Artimatrix and Faux Effects® International for being the first to support the project when it was only a concept with absolutely no guarantee of success.

My friends Suzanne Leedy and Susie Darrell-Smith not only served as board members but also kept me fed and sane during the process. Thanks to Cynthia Paul for introducing me to the business and to my good friends Ernie Dominguez and family, Mike and Peg San Roman, Barb and Vic Tise, Roger Dimsdale, John and Maureen Dubia, Kim Wadford, and Barb Trent for providing critical emotional support.

I also owe a very deep note of gratitude to those who helped me to develop the leadership skills and courage to take on such a project: Dean Larry Wilson and Montreat College, SGM Jimmie Spencer, SGM Don Airhart, MSG Ray Wilson, LTC Darrell Best, Col William L. Hart, Col John Spears, LTG Tom Plewes, LTG John Pickler, Richard and Vicki Scherberger, Col Crissy Gayagas, Gen. and Mrs. Denny Reimer and MG Wallace.

Mentors often include those in the media. Many books and personalities have made a major impact on the way I view the world: Wayne Dyer (You'll See it When You Believe It, No Limit Person, etc), Joe Dominguez and Vicky Robin –(Your Money or Your Life) Oprah Winfrey (Inspirational Shows and her life and spirit in general), HGTV (home makeover ideas) Dr. Phil-(get real), Martha Stewart and Andrea Stoddard (how to make the everyday beautiful.) Anthony Robins (Books on tape series), Robert Redford (Building Sundance / ongoing environmental work) our library system for a world of free art education, and to my publisher, and particular thanks to Marilyn Ross and Vicky Nuttall for getting me to press.

Last but not least, a special note of thanks to my family: Sadly two of my four brothers-Leo & Bill died just as the house was nearing completion, Leo in a skiing accident & Bill of a heart attack. My mother, going through a difficult transition herself, had to put up with 12 months of my absence due to total involvement in this project. Thanks for understanding, Mom. My brother Robert and his partner Elly in Holland have always inspired me with their incredible creativity and ability to make a house a home–even when that "house" is a sailboat. My honorary brother, Gary, is not only supportive but is like human Prozac–he can't help but lift one's spirits.

The Passmanns, my adoptive family, have shared 25 magical German Christmases in their ultimate loving, warm and cozy home. While no longer alive, my father instilled in me the ability to take risks, not to fear the unknown and just jump right in.

Last, John David, my twin brother and Priest of The Church of the Atonement for letting us use his church as a pallet. Having often been on the receiving end of my overzealous creativity, he was somewhat dubious, yet allowed us to add his church and rectory to the project in order to accommodate a greater number of talented artists. In the end, of course, he was thrilled... and yes, I think a bit surprised.

—Adrienne van Dooren

Why We Did It

These images remind of us the incredible force of nature that flattened much of Louisiana and the adjacent states. While much has been done to rebuild the area, there is still an overwhelming amount of building and repair still needed.. Sales of this book and how-to DVDs will fund one or more homes to be built in New Orleans. Over half the money required for the first house has already been raised through home tours and sales of the special edition book.

If you'd like to get involved on the house in New Orleans or our next Artists4Others project/book, email us at www.fauxhouse.com. While there, sign-up for a free quarterly newsletter identifying volunteer opportunities, capturing new projects in photos, and offering new tips and how-to's. and contests.

Photographer, Craig Morse, moved to New Orleans to capture the challenges and changes. See more of his incredible New Orleans Photography at:www.flickr.com/photos/culturesubculture/sets or email him at: csc.foto@gmail.com

Foreword

To say that The House that Faux Built has been a salutary experience for me would be a grave understatement on many levels. Adrienne's initial conception for this project -to redo a fixer upper in support of Habitat for Humanity was during one of our many "happy hour wine and canapé" evenings. Needless to say it seemed like the most perfect idea she had ever had! Little did we all realize that this was one of the things that she would remember the next day, simply because she had been determined to do it in the first place and had used our gathering as the forum to float the idea.

When I first saw the house that she had chosen, my heart sank, while it was in a very good neighborhood it was expensive, particularly unattractive and sorely lacking (in my opinion) the potential required to turn it into the masterpiece Adrienne had envisioned. Needless to say I voiced my opinions strongly to the other Board members and into several glasses of wine over the following weeks! I refused to visit the house to view the work in progress, (as it turns out denying myself the opportunity of meeting amazing artists who had traveled nationally and internationally) insisting to Adrienne that I was "saving myself for the finished product!"

That day finally came. As we parked at the house I was immediately overwhelmed by the new look of the exterior including, but not limited to, the new landscaping, path leading to the front door, new look of the shed, stairs leading to the back entrance, the fountain and essentially the wonderful ambiance and overall peaceful feeling that this engendered. All this before I had even entered the house!

Suffice it to say that I have never experienced the overwhelming emotion that literally left me speechless as I toured the house. Each and every room, hallway, closet and bathroom is truly an exercise in artistic triumph. Each time I thought that I had seen the most magnificent work possible and I moved on to the next area I was, yet again, proven wrong!

This house is a living, breathing, breathtaking example of an inspired and humanitarian idea by Adrienne van Dooren, and brought to life by the top artists nationally and internationally, who so generously gave of their amazing talents and time. The project also serves as a symbol of the incredible possibilities for the rebirth of the homes in the hurricane damaged southern states.

—Susie Darrell-Smith

Before

The FP seemed tall for the room & sconces were lost on the wall

Before

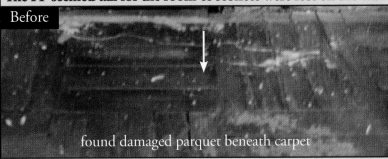

found damaged parquet beneath carpet

Wood parquet was stained and water damaged

What we did:

- *Painted over red brick fireplace*
- *Troweled Quartzstone™ over hearth*
- *Added over-mantel*
- *Glazed ceiling*
- *Troweled lime marmorino on walls*
- *Removed carpet to expose wood floor*
- *Sanded and bleached damaged parquet*
- *Painted/distressed doors, trim and mantle*
- *Stained floor to look like inlay wood*

Living Room
From 40's to Fabulous

The living room should be the heart of the home, but this room seemed cold and dated. The brick fireplace, red ceramic hearth and old fashioned front door screamed 1940's. Poor color choices added to the problem. The harsh contrast between the white ceiling and trim, yellow walls and cool toned gray carpet made the room seem stark and small.

Barth White of Las Vegas was selected to transform this space. While best known for his work in grand casinos such the Belagio, he tackled this tiny space with equal flair.

The primary objectives for the room were to: add warmth, use eco-friendly materials, update the space, and to make the room appear larger.

Barth and his team first prepared and primed the fireplace, then glazed the brick in a soft trio of metallic glazes. The red ceramic-tile hearth was updated by troweling on 4 thin layers of Quartz-stone™ leaving a bit of texture. The plaster is made with real quartz, stable at high temperatures and dries to be very hard and durable. Once glazed, the hearth looks and feels like a real stone slab. Now, this cozy living room invites you to sit and relax by the fire.

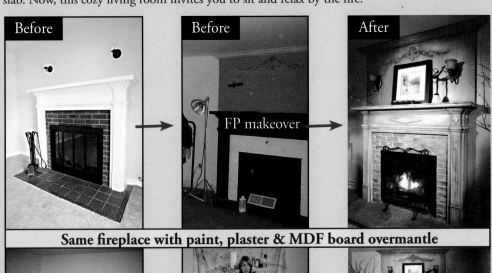

Before — **Before** — **After** — FP makeover

Same fireplace with paint, plaster & MDF board overmantle

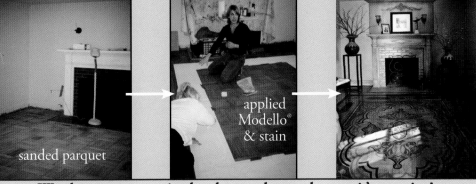

sanded parquet — applied Modello® & stain

Wood parquet was stained and water-damaged—now it's stunning!

Custom stencil with lime paint

Resin Trim Piece

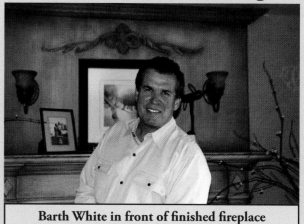

Barth White in front of finished fireplace

The palette of golden earth tones was custom mixed to complement the warm wood tones of the floor. The walls were plastered with a natural lime based marmorino by Rivedil™. While labor intensive, marmorino imparts an aged Italian feel to the room, providing a warmth impossible to mimic with paint.

In progress

At this stage the walls and brick FP have been primed and wood/trim added above the mantle

White door was painted, crackled and distressed

Spraying the ceiling

Barth and his team painted the door, mantle and trim dark brown, then applied Adicolor Crackle Medium in certain areas, followed by a lighter overcoat of paint and antiquing glaze. Once dry, Barth used sandpaper to uncover areas of dark brown in raised areas for a naturally aged appearance. His trim color is only slightly darker than the walls, thus unifying the room.

To further soften the room and make the ceiling appear higher, Barth matched a paint and glaze mixture to the wall color and applied it to the white ceiling with a HVLP sprayer. He used his signature Faux Tool to blend the glaze quickly and efficiently.

Before

View from Living Room Toward Side Porch & Kitchen

This before shot of the living room wall (opposite the fireplace) illustrates the power of paint and plaster to completely transform a space from cold and boring to warm and wow! The new color choices tie together the living room, hall and kitchen and create a harmonious flow to this open floor plan.

The living room makeover proves that the right color scheme can make a small room look larger and challenges the common myth that white ceilings make a room look taller. See our tips to making the most of small spaces in the last chapter.

After

Piecing together the Modello®

Melanie Royals applying stain

Saving the Damaged Parquet Floor

The living room floor was covered with gray-blue carpet. While worn, the carpet was in better shape than the wood floor beneath. Over the years of multiple rentals, the floor had suffered from water damage, grime, pet stains and dripped paint. It was in such bad shape that a professional floor finishing company deemed it beyond repair and stated the only alternative was to replace it.

Unwilling to rip out the original parquet if there was any hope, Ann Bayer and husband Carl decided to tackle it. By sanding and then applying wood bleach, they were able to lessen the contrast between the dark pet stains and lighter woods. They then applied wood putty to fill the cracks. This was followed by more sanding, a sealer and light stain.

Melanie Royals, artist, author and founder of Modello Designs® flew from San Diego and taught a group of volunteers how to apply a 6' x 8' Modello Decorative Masking Pattern®. The one-time-use, adhesive vinyl stencil was custom sized to fit the room. Modellos® have revolutionized the faux world by allowing intricate patterns to be produced less expensively and on a large scale. Further, the self adhesive prevents against the bleed under that can be problematic when using mylar stencils.

Once the pattern was applied to the floor, Melanie and her team of volunteers used water-based gel Stain and Seal® to stencil the various colors through the elaborate pattern.

Was it worth it? While a huge amount of work, the reward was an eco-friendly and truly unique patterned floor plus a huge sense of accomplishment.

Artists & Sponsors

Artists:

Barth White - walls, door, mantle, ceiling and trim
Melanie Royals - faux inlay floor and Modello® class
Anne Bayer - Room Captain, hearth and table
Stuart Kershner - overmantle, grates and moldings
Carl Bayer - floor preparation
Debbie Thompson - picture framing
Team Members - Sandi Anderson, Melissa Clements, Tania Seabock, Rosalie Myers, Rebecca Hotop, Sandra Davis, Mitch Eanes, and Pauline Siple.

Designers:

Nancy AtLee and Mau-Don Nuyen

Sponsors:

Arlington Paint & Decorating Center - painting supplies
Barth White - the Faux Tool™
Beaux-Artes - decorative vents, moldings and FP topper
Color Wheel - Benjamin Moore, Adicolor, and Lime Seal
Decorator's Supply Warehouse - composite molding piece
Dominion Floors - final sealing of floors
Faux and Fleur Designs - hand painted table
Faux Effects® International - Stain & Seal™, Quartzstone™, FX Thinner™ and sealers
Hanging Treasures - frames
Mann Brothers - Casein
Mixol™ - tints
Modello Designs® - floor decorative masking pattern
    The Faux School - Rivedil™, Amaze-a-Glaze™ wall and ceiling products
Voss Creative - custom stencil
Westover Florist - fresh flowers

After / Before
Parquet floor was stained and water-damaged

Before
Ann & Carl Bayer sanding floor

After
Parquet now looks like expensive inlay

After
Console stained to match floor

6

Photo by Omar Selinas

Before

Brick porch becomes an elegant dining room

Before **After**

Cement is _painted_ to look like wood and marble!

Dining Room

A seldom used brick porch becomes an elegant dining room. The view and natural flow from indoor living areas to the outdoor patio made this room ideally suited for a party buffet station or a romantic dinner for two.

After

Photo by Omar Selinas

"Etched" glass is _painted_

This side porch was unattractive and used mainly for storage. It was unusable in winter because the 1940's windows offered no insulation. However, its close proximity to the kitchen and the BBQ area made it perfect for entertaining. By adding new windows and weatherproofing materials around the door and beadboard, the room can now be used year round. The bay window makes the room seem far more spacious.

What we did:

- *Painted cement floor*
- *Covered beadboard trim and wood grained the panels*
- *Glued-on trim pieces and finished in gold leaf*
- *Wood grained white trim to resemble rich walnut*
- *Covered beadboard ceiling with canvas*
- *Plastered over brick*
- *Replaced oversized fan*
- *Replaced drafty windows with energy efficient ones*
- *Molded a new window sill*
- *Stenciled paint on windows for etched look*

Before

Canvas covers bead-board

Glued-on molding

To cover the beadboard ceiling, Tania painted a mural on heavy canvas using pigments mixed with acrylic medium. The beautiful micro-mosaic pattern utilizes curves to contrast with the square patterned floor. It took several volunteers and extra heavy duty construction adhesive to mount the heavy canvas to the ceiling. Inexpensive 1 x 4 inch trim placed along the ceiling hides the edges and gives the look of a tray ceiling.

Photo by Omar Selinas

It's not burl–It's painted!

The dated bead-board was updated by adding insulation, a thin sheet of recycled plastic, and lightweight Spanish Empire ornaments from Beaux-Artes. The plastic was then painted to mimic expensive carved burled wood. The ornamentation was highlighted with gold leaf.

Hand-molded window sill

This window sill looks and feels like marble but was hand molded by Tania Seabock using Scagliola (Sca-li-o-la). This old world European technique was invented in the 1500's to imitate Pietra Dura (inlay stones). Tania created a mold and poured in a mixture of plaster, rabbit skin glue, pigment, and lime, creating a beautiful swirl of colors to complement the ceiling. She then sanded until smooth and sealed with linseed oil.

Shimmering sage Lusterstone™ covers brick

Beaux-Artes hinge-straps are simply glued adjacent to existing hinges for an added decorative element. They come in many styles and finishes and can make an old door look new and elegant.

Hinge Strap

Modello® stencils and specialty craft paints were used to create frosted "etched" glass designs.

A Beaux-Artes door knob escutcheon was glued around the existing knob for an easy and elegant custom look.

Escutcheon over old door knob

This faux inlay marble and wood floor was painted over the existing concrete and sealed well to withstand foot traffic. The warm wood tones tie in with the trim. The grid pattern makes the room appear larger. A how-to DVD for this floor is available through our website.

Not marble and wood–painted!

9

Photo by Omar Selinas

faux matchbook →

Painted matchbook --visitors try to pick it up

blue painter's tape

Painter's tape was used to create the floor pattern

Matchbook: New Orleans artist, Ashley Spencer, painted a New Orleans matchbook to remind visitors of the purpose of the HTFB project. The matchbook is so realistic, even the other artists tried to pick it up.

Walls: To seal and smooth the brick walls, we combined a mixture of Dry-loc™ moisture sealing paint and 90-minute drywall powder. This inexpensive mixture makes a very strong plaster. We then added Versiplast™ followed by several layers of Lusterstone™ shimmering plaster in a mix of olive and champagne mist gold. The walls now have a beautiful shimmer and perfectly complement the silk curtain. In hindsight it would have been far less work to have applied drywall panels directly to the brick wall with screws and construction adhesive. Lusterstone™ looks best on a perfectly smooth wall and we spent days getting it smooth.

Floor: Designed to visually enlarge the room and complement the door's glass panels, the squares also provide a nice contrast to the curves of the ceiling mural. Tania masked out the marble pattern with 1/8th and 1 inch painter's tape. She used the classic European method of creating realistic woods and marbles with beer and pigment for the first layer followed by artist's paints. Tania painted the large squares in a faux gray breche marble and the accent pieces in yellow sienna. Once dry, she re-taped the floor and completed the wood-graining process. The floor took a total of five days to complete.

Tania's how to DVD is available through www.fauxhouse.com

Artists & Sponsors

Room Captain Tania Seabock beginning the wood grain.

Artists:

Tania Seabock - Room Captain, wood graining, floor, ceiling, windowsill, gilding, icon
Carol Patterson - Room Lieutenant, Lusterstone™ walls
Nicola Vigini - grottesca panel
Adrienne van Dooren - general design and color choices
Rebecca Hotop - frosted Modello® window patterns and Lusterstone™ walls
Stuart Kershner - Spanish wainscotting and ornamentation
Ashley Spencer - trompe' l oeil matchbook
Ceil Glembocki - window treatments and flower arrangements
Maria Zannette - window treatment installation
Ian Seabock - scaglliola
Team Members - Sean Bessenyei, Steve Brown, John Lenard, Hector Lopez, Caroline Spencer and Lisa Turner

Sponsors:

Andreae Stencils® - large trowels and brushes
Arlington Paint and Decorating Center - paint, varnish and supplies
Art Stuf - mold making materials, plasters, waxes, fiberglass, pigments and adhesives
Beaux-Arts - composite ornament, door hinge straps and door escutcheon
Calico Corners - window treatment hardware and decorative tassels
Color Wheel - Benjamin Moore® Paints and Versiplast™
Discount Fabrics USA® - drapery fabric
Faux Effects International - Lusterstone™ and supplies
Faux Fingers - small trowels for plaster application
Golden Artist Colors Inc®. - paints -acrylic ground for pastels, absorbent ground and acrylic modifier for plaster
Plaza Arts - paints, brushes and other necessary items
Royal Design Studio® - panel design stencils for side windows
Sinopia - raw powdered pigments, gold leaf, and artist's brushes
Steve Brown Construction - trim
Modello Designs® - decorative masking pattern for small window panes
Thompson Creek Windows - energy efficient replacement windows including bay windows and copper roof on the bay window.
Vigini Studios - donated panel

After

Before

Removed partial wall

3/4 wall to dining room

Same Refrigerator,
Dishwasher
& Cabinetry!

Before

Could not open fridge door without hitting oven

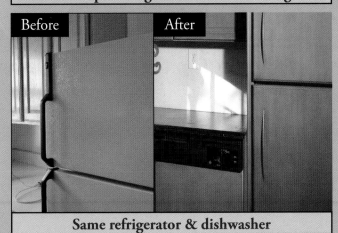

Before / After

Same refrigerator & dishwasher

Before / After

Partial wall removed to expand kitchen into old dining room

What we did:

- Removed 3/4 wall (non-load bearing)
- Combined kitchen and old dining room
- Painted dishwasher panel
- Added panels and handles to refrigerator
- Troweled concrete floor in faux flagstone
- Plastered walls and fauxed ceiling
- Painted cabinets
- Plastered countertops
- Created faux tile backsplash
- Added window treatments and light fixtures
- Replaced old stove
- Built bench seat with storage

Floor Plans

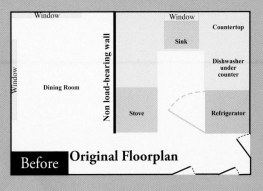

Window | Window | Countertop | Sink | Dishwasher under counter | Stove | Refrigerator | Non load-bearing wall | Window | Dining Room

Before — **Original Floorplan**

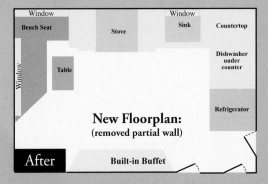

Window | Window | Bench Seat | Stove | Sink | Countertop | Dishwasher under counter | Table | Refrigerator | Window

New Floorplan:
(removed partial wall)

After — **Built-in Buffet**

The **tiny kitchen** and disfunctional dining room were separated by a 3/4 wall. By removing the wall, we combined the two rooms into a larger eat-in kitchen.

Older kitchens can be made new with faux. Had we not needed the additional space, everything could have been fauxed in place.

Disruption and expense was minimized by keeping the cabinets and all the appliances except the stove. The stove could have been painted with special heat resistant paint, but it was large and dated so we opted for a new energy efficient stainless steel model which could serve as a central focal point.

The cabinets and dishwasher were painted and the refrigerator customized by attaching routed MDF board, new handles and paint. Adding Krylon® magnetic paint additive ensures artwork and notes can still be hung on the door.

Caroline Woldenberg of The Finishing Source, Inc. (Atlanta) is both an interior designer and an expert faux finisher. She designed the kitchen makeover based upon her experiences visiting and working in European kitchens. The spaces were often small but served as the heart of the home. She was particularly impressed by the centuries old walls which bore witness to the passage of time; yet, despite the well worn surfaces, were clean and comfortable, encouraging one to linger over a meal.

After

Glazed Ceiling

Window Boxes

Plastered Walls

$10 Yardsale Table

Faux Flagstone

Painted Stock Cabinets & Added Trim

Plastered Counter Tops

Colors: Caroline carefully selected colors to create old world warmth. The walls and ceiling were glazed in yellow ochre tones, the cabinetry in Italian sienna and the trim in teal. The complementary teal trim brings excitement to this small kitchen, giving every detail more emphasis and visual impact.

Walls: Caroline and her team applied O'Villa™ wall plaster using a stainless steel trowel in a vertical technique to emphasize height and make the ceiling seem higher. They aged the newly plastered walls using RS Series™ glaze and activator by Faux Effects® International.

Ceiling: Matching the ceiling glaze to the wall colors makes the ceiling appear taller since there is no harsh line between the wall color and a white ceiling. You won't find a white ceiling in the faux house.

Cabinets: By purchasing 6 additional builder's grade cabinets from Lowes and rearranging those we had, costs were kept to a minimum. Caroline chose to top the cabinets with inexpensive wood molding and stagger the height for a custom look. She also brought forward the cabinets on the left and right of the stove and above the refrigerator to make the appliances look built-in.

Floor: The faux "flagstone" floor was created by DC Concrete Technology. They began by removing the old linoleum from the kitchen and carpet from dining room exposing the cement floor beneath. By taping off an irregular pattern they created the "grout" pattern and then troweled on a tinted cement overlay . Once they pulled up the tape the "stone" was raised and textured resembling real flagstone. The cement was tinted in pale sienna tones which further warm and unify the room.

14

In progress

Caroline used tape and marmarino plaster to create a backsplash of very convincing faux tile

In progress

She added Venetian plaster diamonds to match the countertop and tie together the two spaces

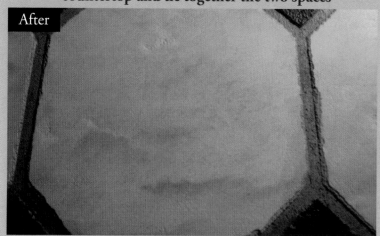

After

Looks like granite but can go right over old Formica™

Countertops
Remodeling doesn't have to mean ripping out.

◀ Wanda Timmons of Designer Finishes, Illinois, sponged Venetian Gem™ plaster in black, topaz and gold in multiple layers, each time knocking it down with a trowel. She then glazed over the entire counter top with earth brown aqua color™ acrylic paint mixed with water to unify the colors, creating a very realistic faux granite. These counter tops were made of inexpensive plywood and trim, however, this finish can also be used over properly prepared Formica. Wanda applied a brown glaze to tie the colors together and several coats of sealer to protect the finish. A new inexpensive but stylish faucet completes the update. Wanda has put together a how-to DVD on making over counter tops available on our website.

Dan Mahlmann and Gary Arvanitopulos ▶ finished this buffet-style counter top to resemble stone. They troweled a cement overlay over wood and finished it with epoxy. The faux "inlay" strip was taped off and tinted in sienna tones to complement the cabinetry. The buffet cabinets were actually the original upper cabinets in the before photo above the dishwasher. The 12" depth was perfect for this narrow passage area. Small wooden shelves were added on either end for a more built-in look. The beautiful grotesca canvas hanging on the wall above the buffet was painted in Umbria, Italy by artist Nicola Vigini.

Cement over wood

The countertop is inexpensive wood coated with cement and placed over the original upper cabinets we painted and moved to the floor

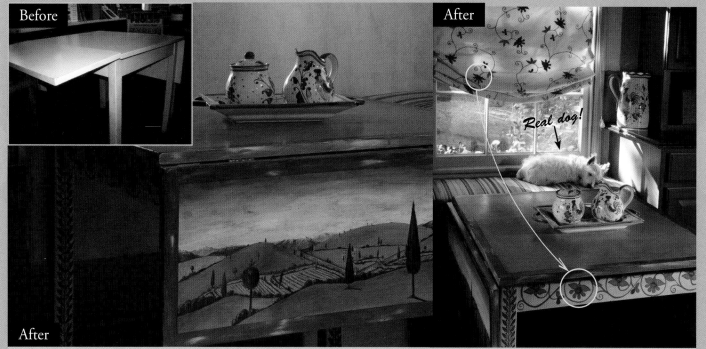

Before

After

After

Real dog!

$10 yard sale table painted to match both the curtain design and the Tuscan theme of the room

Patti Irwin of Maryland took this $10 yard sale table and turned it into a treasure. She used casien milk based paints and distressed the finish by sanding, thus creating an instant heirloom. The table is perfectly sized for the small kitchen but can be expanded for guests. Patti matched the colors and the pattern of the curtain fabric on each side of the table. She created a similar vine and leaf design for the table legs. The table top's sienna tones complement the kitchen cabinetry, while each table leaf portrays a painted scene from the Tuscan countryside. The table ties in perfectly with the overall Italian feel of the kitchen.

Caroline and her team spent many hours preparing the cabinets and box seat to make them perfectly smooth before painting. They first deglossed the cabinets, then applied Master Finishing Medium™ to fill the wood grain and sanded using fine grit sandpaper. They painted the cabinets with a 4-stage sprayer and Setcoat™, a self leveling, long lasting basecoat and primer in one. An antiquing glaze coupled with subtle striae and splatter give the cabinets a rich, timeless finish.

Normal builder's cabinets and wood were all that was needed for this "custom" kitchen

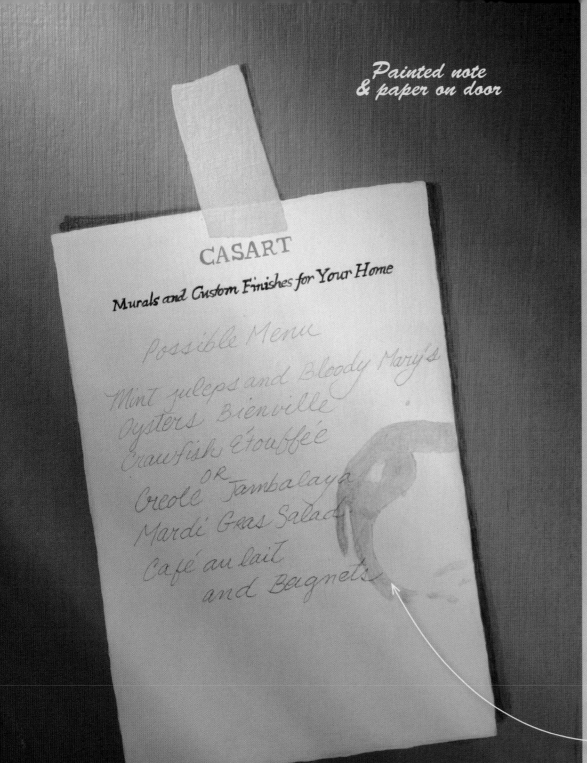

Painted note
& paper on door

CASART

Murals and Custom Finishes for Your Home

Possible Menu

Mint juleps and Bloody Mary's
Oysters Bienville
Crawfish Étouffée
OR
Creole Jambalaya
Mardi Gras Salad
Café au lait
and Beignets

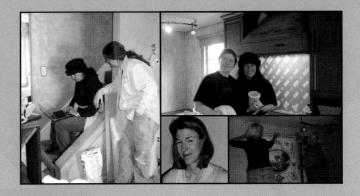

Artists:

Caroline Woldenberg - Room Captain and Designer
Amanda Summerlin – Co-Room Captain
Wanda Timmons – Venetian plaster counter top
Dan Mahlmann – cement overlay counter top
Gary Arvanitopulos – cement overlay counter top
Nicola Vigini – grotesca panel
Ashley Spencer – trompe l'oeil note
Patti Irwin – kitchen table
Team Members: Jenny Vanier–Walter, Maureen M. Watkins, Carolyn Spencer, Carol Patterson, Debbie Dennis, Julie Miles, Kimberly Bohn, Carl Bayer, Russell Sellineer, Reginald Flemming, Lewis Lewis, Sheri Anderson, Sandra Davis, Susan Huber, Pauline Sipple, Ceil Glembocki, Stuart Kershner, Robin Bear, and Shireen Balkissoon

Sponsors:

Arlington Paint & Decorating Center - supplies
Beaux-Artes - vent cover and refrigerator panels
Bray and Scarff - loan of stainless steel stove
Calico Corners - window treatments & bench seat cushions
DC Concrete Technologies - floor materials
Faux Effects International - paints, plasters, material and sealers
Hanging Treasures - frames
Krylon Paints - magnetic and chalkboard paints
Decorative Concrete of Maryland, Inc - counter top materials
Michael Gross - trash can
The Finishing Source, Inc, Atlanta - materials

The note, tape and even the "coffee stain" were painted on the kitchen door by New Orleans artist, Ashley Spencer. The Creole menu reminds visitors of the purpose of the project

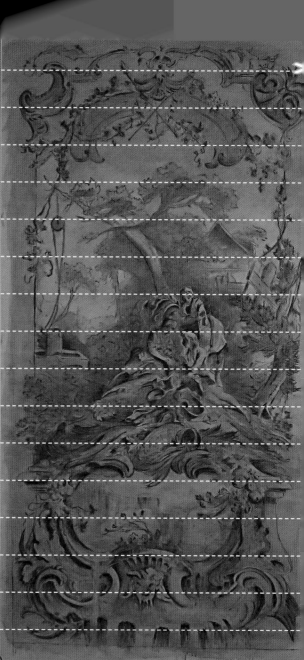

Mural was cut in strips and glued to face of steps

What we did:

- *Chose a book / library theme*

- *Removed old carpet to reveal wood*

- *Painted, cut, and installed cartouch*

- *Painted diamond pattern on stairs*

- *Embedded book quotations in plast*

- *Painted quoted books in painted bo*

- *Created a cosy reading nook*

- *Painted library mural for base of st*

- *Painted trompe l'oeil niche*

After

Before

After

Murals add interest and visually expand the space

In progress

Painter's tape, Stain & Seal, and Behr porch paint were used to create floor pattern

Actual dog toy & bowl add realism and depth to the mural

Attic access panel painted to

The floor: The old grey carpet was removed to reveal the oak beneath. Artist Amy Ketteran dressed up the wooden steps with a hand-painted cartouche and harlequin diamonds. She painted the cartouche in her Maryland studio, choosing sepia tone on tone to complement the red oak. Amy later cut the mural into 14 strips and pasted them to the face of the steps with clay adhesive. Two coats of sealer help protect against scuff marks.

She finished the top of each step and the upper landing with a diamond pattern. Amy used Stain & Seal to bring out the richness of the wood and Behr Porch Paint for the diamonds. Once dry, she sanded the diamonds to age and distress them. As a result, the floor feels original to the home.

The murals: The trompe l'oeil niche, sky-light, bookshelves and library scene were also painted in Amy's studio and installed on site. The mural at the base of the steps gives the illusion of depth as visitors descend the stairs because it appears there is

Before

Unused space between two hall closets

Top of Stairwell:
imbedded quotes in wall finish contribute to library theme

After

Cozy reading nook

After

Vent allows air circulation

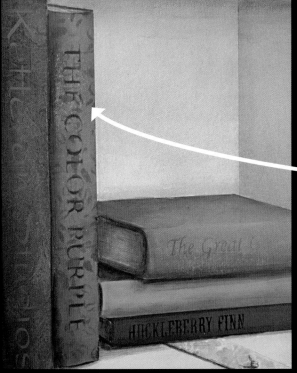

Quoted books *are painted in bookshelves (e.g. The Color Purple)*

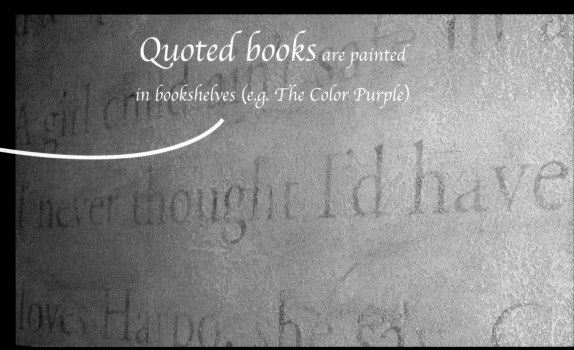

The Color Purple painted in a faux book shelf

Quotations from *The Color Purple, Huckleberry Finn*, etc. are imbedded in the wall

Cozy reading nook

In Progress

The **walls** also reflect the library theme. Quotations from the classics are imbedded in the wall. Faux artist Andra Held used "Say What™" one-time-use adhesive word stencils to add quotations on the walls using bronze metallic paint and Aquastone™ to create this look. She sanded over the words so they appear faded and aged. A final glaze provides a slight metallic glow.

In Progress

"Say What™ adhesive stencils make lettering easy.

This finish would have been incredibly time-consuming if we'd had to use traditional lettering stencils or tracings.

Say What can create custom lettering in any font, size and even perfectly sized arches.

Painted bookshelf

Faux dog

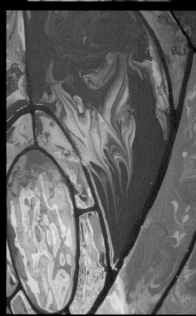

Faux Stained Glass is Really Painted Plexiglas

▲ Faux stained glass:

Plexiglas and specialty paints were used to make faux stained glass. The faux leading was made with tinted drywall joint-compound. The design brings out the colors of the fabric and serves as a focal point as you climb the stairs.

◄ The Westie shown left fooled visitors who often petted him before realizing he was stuffed. Reactions were strong as folks either loved it or were disturbed by it. The dog, Titan, was preserved by KeepMyPet.com after a tragic accident. They use a special freeze drying method which, unlike taxidermy, preserves the "personality" of the pet.

26

A Boring Landing is Now a Cozy Reading Nook

Before

Before

After

Reading Nook: The top of the stairs was a family affair; Amy's husband built a cozy reading nook in the opening between two hall closets and her mother sewed cushions and window treatments. The window seat lifts up for storage. Amy applied gold leaf to the decorative vent, door hardware, mirrors, and banister.

Doors Transformed with Antiqued Mirrors

Before

In progress

After

Mirror glued to doors

Door Transformation: Amy had regular mirrors cut to the size of the door panels. She chemically removed the black paint from the back. Using an antique mirror patina solution kit, she distressed and aged the mirror. Then she applied a Modello® adhesive stencil and removed the silver backing from the exposed areas of the stencil and replaced it with gold paint. Once dry, she painted the entire back of the mirror with a partial coat of brown spray paint followed by 2 coats of black spray paint and a shellac sealer. The mirrors were attached in the door panels using mastic and make the small hall look more spacious and elegant.

Artists
&
Sponsors

Artists:

Amy Ketteran - Room Captain/Murals
Andra Held - Faux Finisher
Team Members - Sandra Davis, Joan Hagan, Mark Ketteran, Pauline Siple, Caroline Spencer, Francesca Springolo, Karen Steele, and Chris Woodruff

Sponsors:

ASPS Industries Inc - mirror kit
Behr® - porch paint
Dominion floors - final floor finish
Faux Effects® International - Aquastone, Stain & Seal, wall finish/ sealing products
Keepmypet.com - preserved pet
Plaza Arts - Delta and Plaid metallic paints
Modello® Designs - decorative masking pattern for mirror
"Say What" Stencils - adhesive word stencils

Glazed ceiling & mural

Beaded trim

Crackled Venetian plaster

Floor design

Crossroads to Culture

The "Crossroads to Culture" room combines Moroce Moorish, and Indian Designs. The room beckons you and immerse yourself in the magic of the East

Before

What we did:

- Plastered 2 walls in crackled Venetian plaster
- Plastered 2 walls in smooth VP with imbedded de
- Applied gold wax over plaster
- Removed carpet and stenciled wood floor
- Replaced ceiling fan with small Moroccan light
- Fauxed ceiling and added design to complement f
- Woodgrained doors and trim
- Installed window scene mural
- Fauxed and decorated closet
- Added beaded trim

Crackled Venetian plaster with gold wax

Ron Layman chose a beautiful Rivedil™ Venetian plaster for the walls. He created two accent walls by using a crackle medium under the final layer of plaster. Once the cracks formed, he applied gold wax to define the cracks and soften the wall color. For the opposite walls he chose a smooth finish. However, for added interest, he imbedded a Moroccan design by stenciling it between the first and second layer of plaster. For the finishing touch, the designers glued beading from a fabric store around the bedroom's ceiling rather than traditional molding. The beading helped to tie together the colors and enhance the overall multi-cultural theme.

Smooth plaster with imbedded designs

After–Day

The ceiling, or
"5th wall" is too often
ignored by homeowners. In
this case the white ceiling would
have seemed too harsh and cold against
the red walls. Therefore Ron fauxed the ceiling
with wax tinted in subtle warm earth tones. The ceiling
design was stenciled on canvas using a smaller Modello® in the same
design as the floor. Replacing the large ceiling fan with a smaller light makes the
room appear larger. The red glass casts a lustrous red light pattern across the ceiling, which, when it deepens at night, has a truly magical feel and unites the red
walls and earth-toned ceiling.

After–Night

The Floor

In progress

Ron adhering Modello® to floor

Henna-colored stain

Doors & Trim

Before

After

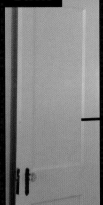

Before

In progress

After

White doors and trim were wood-grained

The bedroom was all white including trim and doors. The white trim would not have complemented the new red walls. In fact, no paint color would have given the same warmth of wood.

Artists Mike Bedster of England and John Leonard of Arlington, VA used European beer based wood graining techniques to simulate beautiful and rare wood. The result is luminous and totally convincing. The graining was accomplished in several layers to achieve depth. John ensured the wood was perfectly smooth and applied a straw yellow basecoat. Mike painted the grain used primarily artists brushes as shown above.

The Mural

This acrylic-on-canvas mural was painted at the International Salon of Decorative Artists by four respected and accomplished artisans: Pascal Amblard, Sean Crosby, Pierre Finkelstein and Nicola Vigini. This original composition depicts a seated figure in a traditional sari overlooking a tranquil landscape in Northern India. The woman depicted in the panel is the wife of muralist Sean Crosby.

Landscape murals are a great way to visually expand space and make a small room appear larger. If original artwork is outside your price-range, canvas prints or treated paper murals are a less expensive alternative. If you'd like to paint one yourself, Sean and Pascal teach similar composition classes at The Mural school and have produced how-to DVDs available through our website.

Mural enlarges space

Artists:

Ronald Layman - Room Captain
Tracy Weir - Co-Room Lieutenant
Lisa Turner - Co-Room Lieutenant
John Leonard - wood graining prep and support
Mike Bedster (England) - wood graining
Sean Crosby - combined mural panel
Pascal Amblard - combined mural panel
Nicola Vigini - combined mural panel
Pierre Finkelstein - combined mural panel
Deborah Thompson - stretched canvas mural
Mau-Don Nuyen - Designer
Nancy AtLey - Designer

Sponsors:

Arlington Paints and Decorating - paints & supplies
Curtains, Upholstery and Furniture, LLC-furniture
Hanging treasures - stretched mural on frame
Hotop Family – donated moroccan table
The Faux School - Terra I'Talia, Décor Fondo, Rivedil™
The Mural School - Indian woman in a window mural
Modello Designs® - decorative masking patterns

33

Before

In progress

Deb Drager applying plaster directly over the shower tile

In progress

Deb and Donna making faux "windows"

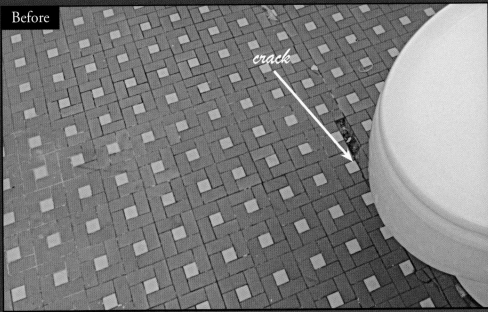

crack

Crack and hole were covered with sparkling plaster for a faux slate look

Master Bath

Original tiled bathroom is now a small Moroccan retreat with beautiful "carved stone" elements

Before

After

plastered over this tile

What we did:

- *Troweled Lusterstone™ "slate" finish <u>over</u> floor tile*

- *Replaced toilet seat and sink with faux stone versions*

- *Covered white shower tile with faux stone plaster*

- *Applied gilded palm finish to walls and ceiling*

- *Added faux windows and painted sky behind tub*

- *Updated old mirror with mosaic tile*

- *Glued light weight faux stone panel to front of tub*

- *Finished window trim to resemble textured wood*

Shower Surround is Faux Stone Over Old Tile

The Master Bath: Built in the 1940's, the master bath had never been remodeled. The white tile had yellowed and the grout had darkened over the years. A normal makeover would require ripping out the tub, tile, sink and toilet. Not every homeowner can afford the cost, time and inconvenience of such a remodel. Deb and Donna completed this entire bath in just 3 days! Best of all, this project cost only 20% of what of what a complete remodel would have cost.

Goals:
1. *Update the look*
2. *Make bath seem larger yet cozy*
3. *Tie the bath to the Crossroads to Culture theme*

Before
1940's tile: white, boring and dated

After
Plasters sealed to repel water

After
Faux "windows"

Method: During the course of their research, the artists discovered a wealth of embellishment ideas that fit the bathroom's Moroccan theme. Moroccan architectural elements are filled with pattern within patterns and a variety of designs which Donna and Deb were able to incorporate by using various stencil motifs. They chose neutral earth-tones resembling tumbled marble throughout the middle of the space. There was no need to rip out existing tile. Specialty etching creams, primers, stone-like plasters and sealers enable faux finishers to create a lasting watertight finish. A faux stone sink and toilet seat replaced the old fixtures. The crowning touch to the room is the large Coral-light™ faux stone trim. Incredibly realistic, yet weighing only five pounds, this interior/exterior molded "stone" was easily cut and glued to the tub front. Deb added a faux window and painted sky just above eye level to give the room more visual depth and color. She used various colors of Lusterstone™ to paint the sky and clouds. The shimmering plaster gives the window a reflective quality and lightens up the space.

Donna Phelps using palm leaf stencil on walls and ceiling

Walls and ceilings are gilded palms on shimmering plaster

The artists originally planned to put the palm pattern only on the walls. However, after they examined the space they were so impressed with the unusual curved ceiling that they decided to finish it as well. Placing the large palm patterns on both the walls and ceiling made the ceiling look higher and created a sense of drama. It also visually connected the rest of the room to the faux slate floor, which was covered with the same sage, plus olive and bronze LusterStone™. Placing random large patterns above eye level brings the focus upward for the illusion of height and helps to balance and anchor the room.

Donna Phelps creating a faux silver platter on the wall

The main Moroccan Medallion motif was accomplished with a heavy 14 mil raised plaster stencil from the Victoria Larsen Exclusive Professional Collection. Donna selected this pattern and creatively portrayed it both as carved stone (behind bath) and as a faux silver platter hung from the wall.

After

Before

The 3 "D"s - Donna Phelps, Deb Drager and Donna Smith

Artists:

Deb Drager - Co-Room Captain
Donna Phelps - Co-Room Captain
Donna Smith - Room Lieutenant
Laura Nalley - mosaic mirror
Mau-Don Nuyen and Nancy AtLee - curtains, towels and accessories
Team Members - Steve Brown, Celeste Stewart and Carolyn Spencer

Sponsors:

Artimatrix Academy of Architectural Finishes - materials
Beaux-Artes - decorative grate
Corallight™ (distributed by Artimatrix) - stone front for tub
Faux Effects® International - basecoat, Lusterstone™ and sealers
Lowes - Light and toilet seat
Sarasota School of Faux and Architectural Finishing- materials, tools and stencils
Vintage Homes of Wichita (Anthony Speer) - faucet

After

Before

Painted molding

Upside-down
table legs

Faux tile

Masonite™ hearth

40

Stenciled grotesca design on door panels

"Rug" & "wood" are painted on a floor cloth!

What we did:

- *Added faux fireplace and interchangeable panels*
- *Painted a "tile hearth" on Masonite™*
- *Fauxed walls and ceiling in warm sienna*
- *Hand painted faux molding*
- *Painted furniture and decorative items in cream*
- *Removed carpet to expose wood*
- *Painted floorcloth "rug"*
- *Added scroll work to define curved ceiling*
- *Added ceiling mural*
- *Matched armoire to bedding*

Trompe l'oeil "molding" painted over faux fireplace

41

The Ceiling

The ceiling mural was designed and painted on canvas in the studio and installed on site. An inexpensive chandelier was painted and the small shades decorated with beaded trim to complement the mural.

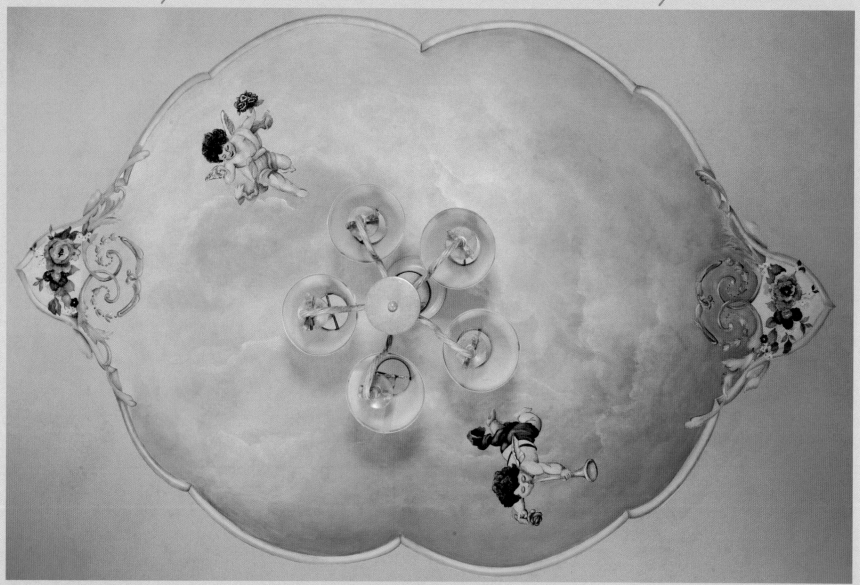

Joanne Nash designed this mural to add height and elegance to the ceiling. The layers of clouds add depth and softness. The painted gold border "molding" looks 3-D and coordinates with the painted moldings around the room. The painted flowers on the points of the mural match the bedding fabric and armoire, further tying the room together.

After

Painted molding

Before

The curved ceiling was unattractive

Painted Details

This room presented four major challenges: its small scale, a curved ceiling on one wall, two very different window sizes, and an awkward placement of doors leading into the hallway and closet. A hand painted ceiling border serves to define the otherwise awkwardly curved ceiling as a distinctive and lovely architectural feature. Joanne chose a warm golden glaze for the walls and ceiling using a chamois cloth for application. She selected pale blue as her accent color to complement the gold and draw the eye around the room.

The carpet was discarded and beautiful hardwood floors were revealed beneath. While some damaged wood had to be replaced, the new wood matches beautifully.

After

Scrollwork makes the strangely-curved ceiling look beautiful

Hand-painted original design

Furniture Make-overs

After

Before

After

Before

Dennis Nash made the single bed and fireplace for the romantic bedroom. The fireplace was made of scrap wood and the hearth from Masonite™ board. The headboard is made of simple MDF board and upside down table legs. Joanne used steam-on composite ornamentation by Decorator's Supply Warehouse on both the headboard and an old humidor table to make them appear to be matched pieces. She primed and painted both in cream and added touches of brown paint with a dry brush to distress the finish.

Joanne found the perfect fabric for the bed throw and accent pillow; however, the colors were too strong and vibrant for the vintage feel. To solve this problem, she soaked the fabric in a mild bleach solution, followed by a solution of tea and water and then dried it in the sun. A salvaged armoire was painted and distressed to match the fabric. As a last detail, Joanne located a ceramic figurine in a thrift store and painted the dress to match the woman in the fabric.

Table-legs & MDF become a headboard

Flowers in ceiling mural

Before

After

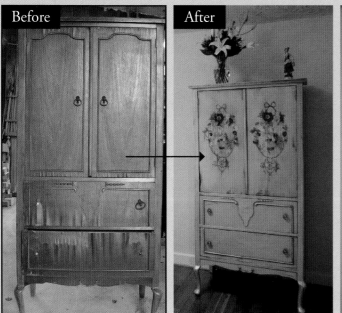

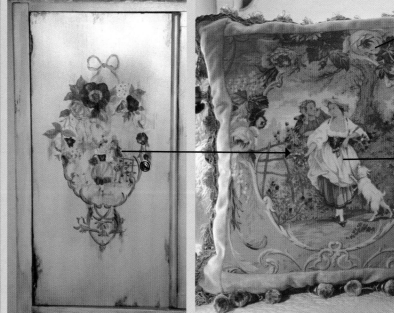

Thrift-store find painted to match fabric

Damaged armoire was painted to match the bedding

In progress

Fireplace built by Dennis Nash

After

Classical panel by Francesca Springolo

Joanne Nash, Adrian Greenfield,
Belinda Yoder and Rebecca Hotop

Artists:

Joanne Nash - Room Captain
Adrian Greenfield - Guest Artist, England
Rebecca Hotop - Room Lieutenant, door, mouse and floor cloth
Kate Nagle - fireplace insert - candles
Francesca Springolo - fireplace insert - classical
Belinda Yoder - window treatments and bedding
Dennis Nash - carpentry, fireplace and bed
Ashley Spencer - romantic closet

Sponsors:

Andreae Stencils - stencils
Beaux-Artes - decorative grate
Cheri Perry - displayed bird house for Noah's Wish auction
Decorator's Supply - add-on molding for furniture
Faux Effects® International - paints, glazes and sealers
Mad Stencilist - wax adhesive
PRO FAUX - JewelStone™ ceiling finish closet, gold wax
Roc-lon, Inc. - canvas for ceiling and floor cloth
Sabina and Sullivan/Discount Fabrics USA - fabrics
Floor repair - Hatcher's Floors

Faux Fireplace: What could be more romantic than a fireplace? Since a real fireplace wasn't an option, Dennis Nash built a mantle and hearth designed to be easily installed and removed without major damage to the wall. Guest artist, Adrian Greenfield of England, painted the primary panel's tile and brick with such realism that many who visited were fooled. To add a touch of whimsy, he painted a Westie sitting inside, apparently ready to play with a ball. The fireplace design allows 3' x 3' canvas inserts to be interchangeable to fit any mood or season. A heated wax adhesive makes it easy to place, adjust, and remove with no mess. Once the wax is applied, it remains tacky and can be repositioned multiple times, even years later. While conducting house tours, we demonstrated replacing the panels several times a day with great success. However, we learned the hard way with the ceiling mural that a hot ceiling light melts wax....oops. For heavier murals, clay wall adhesive was needed. Clay still allows the mural to be removed should the owner move or remodel. Should one not wish to remove the murals, a heavy duty wallpaper adhesive or construction adhesive works well.

After

Burning candles panel by Kate Nagle

After

Dutch tile panel by Adrian Greenfield

Faux tile and brick

Painted tile & brick

Romantic Closet

Ashley Spencer took a boring white closet and added fun trompe l'oeil elements: a painted silk robe, shoes, purses, love letters, a pen and an inkwell. Ashley used stencils for the shoes and purses but hand painted the robe and love letters using real items for reference.

The result is so realistic that many visitors ignored them believing they were real and staged as props. Ashley did add a few real props – a purse, tie, New Orleans beads and padded hangers all add a great deal of depth and aid in the overall illusion.

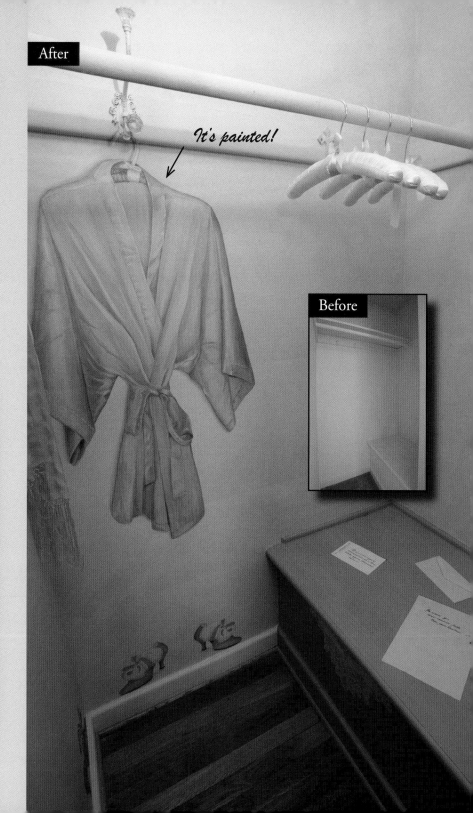

After

It's painted!

Before

Painted!

Painted love letter, envelopes, pen & ink

46

Stenciled & hand painted elements add character to this small space

Before

After

47

Before and after corner

An ethereal feeling was created for the Faux House nursery by using a HVLP sprayer and single action airbrush to paint billowy clouds on the ceiling and walls. These heavenly touches were made courtesy of Melanie Kershener, Artist and Designer for Beaux-Artes Division of Heavenly Home Designs.

The nursery could not officially be considered a third bedroom because it did not have a closet. To solve this problem we bumped a hole through the hall closet into the nursery where we added a small custom door. The closet can now be accessed from both the hall and the nursery. A $100 door increased the value of the home by $10,000!

Walk-in closet becomes third bedroom nursery

Melanie first stenciled this classic mural in acrylics and hand embellished and shaded it for depth. Then she went over the areas she wanted to glow with phosphorescent pigment mixed with water or glaze. The minerals, which can be applied over any color palette, are invisible until the room is dark.

Minerals and fiber-optic curtain glow in the dark

The Nursery

Transformed from a storage closet to a magical land of fairies high above the clouds. It sparkles by day and glows at night

Curtain replaces entrance door /New closet door -right

What we did:

- *Painted the walls, ceiling and floor*
- *Added glow-in-the-dark effect with dark minerals*
- *Glued on faux jewels and "fairy dust"*
- *Created a closet space*
- *Added wooden valances and molding*
- *Made curtains of fiber-optic cloth*
- *Refinished rocking chair and bassinet*
- *Laid down wall-to-wall floorcloth*

Nursery

The room's evening glow acts as a night light which easily allows a mother to nurse her child in the rocking chair. No need to turn on the lights!

The Luminex curtain adds to the ethereal feeling of the nursery. The fiber optics woven into the curtain operate with either AC or battery power.

Day

Rocking chair with pearlescent paints and faux jewels

The bassinet and rocking chair are painted with pearlescent paints. Faux jewels are added to the rocking chair.

The removable lamp shade is adorned with a large faux ruby. It can be used later to top off a princess costume!

Day

The glow-in-the-dark fairies blow crystal "fairy dust" and colorful rhinestone stars into the air.

Night

51

The pearlized closet door uses a drapery tie-back finial as a door knob

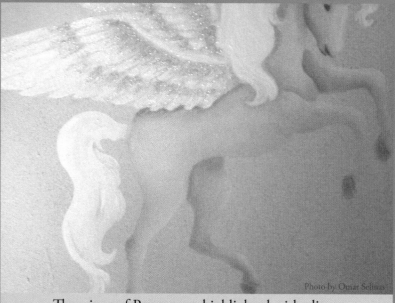

The wings of Pegasus are highlighted with glitter

The hardwood floors in this room were badly stained and would have been expensive to refinish. Had we painted the wood, the slats would have interfered with the illusion of clouds. The decision was made to cover the floor with a wall-to-wall floor cloth secured beneath the molding.

The ceiling, walls and floor are embellished throughout with glow pigment. At night the ceiling comes alive as a galaxy of stars. You can see the city lights of a Mediterranean Isle below the clouds.

Fairies "live" in the floor cloth

Fairies look down through the clouds to the Mediterranean Isles

52

Before

Walk-in closet helps room become an official bedroom

Artists Melanie Kershner and Linda O' Neill spent hours layering colors on the mural

After

Stars, fairies, fairy dust and the fiber optic curtain in this nursery all glow in the dark

Note: fiber-optic curtain needs AC or battery power

The tile floor in the mural of the temple of Hadrian in Ephesus gives depth to the small space. This wall is also visually enlarged through the use of a monochromatic color scheme and by the fact that the colors are wrapped from floor to ceiling. The playful temple fairies are embellished with crystals and rhinestones.

Artists:
Melanie Kershner - Room Captain
Linda O'Neill - Room Lieutenant
Stuart Kershner - installation of moldings, door, grate and cornices
Wanda Swierczynski - sewing bedding for bassinet and curtain
Ceil Glembocki - blackout curtain

Sponsors:
Andreae Stencils™ - garden fairy stencil sets
Buckingham Stencils™ - cornice angels stencil
Beaux-Arts - moldings, vents, door and cornices
Color Wheel - Benjamin Moore paints and Venetian plaster
Faux Effects® International: Basecoat, Pallet Decco™ and Sealers
Heavenly Home Designs - phosphorescent pigments
Modello® - adhesive stencil designs on cornice and doors
Luminex®-Fiberoptic window fabric
Roc-lon® - floor cloth and window shades
Stencil Kingdom - architectural and fairy stencils

In progress   In progress   Before

Arch hides unsightly vent

Wine Cellar

A wine tasting room proved the perfect use for this tiny 6'x8' space; its only other practical use would have been storage.

After

Before

Plastic Barrel

Plastic barrel painted like wooden wine barrel

What we did:

- *Cleaned and sealed concrete walls*
- *Built arch to hide heating vent*
- *Finished ceiling and stairs with drywall*
- *Troweled pitted stone finish on walls and ceiling*
- *Stained eight cheap pine wine cubes*
- *Made countertop of faux tumbled marble*
- *Prepped and stained concrete floor*
- *Added murals and faux stained glass*
- *Painted woodgrain, corks, and broken wine glass*
- *Turned plastic industrial barrel into a table*

Plastic Industrial Barrel: What appears to be a rustic wooden wine barrel is actually a recycled plastic industrial barrel painted by Annie Lemarié, of Main Street Arts. She used Krylon Plastic Primer™ to ensure adhesion and did an incredibly convincing job of wood graining the barrel. The faux "metal" bands, created with painter's tape and Lusterstone™, actually feel like rusted metal. Annie also used Lusterstone™ to create a realistic "slate" top using a circle she cut from a wood scrap. Not a single visitor guessed the barrel wasn't real wood.

Pitted Stone Finish

Visitors feel as if they've descended into a cavern carved from rock, an ambiance perfect for savoring fine wine.

Pitted Stone Wall Finish:

Adrienne selected Kelly King's signature "pitted stone" finish for the walls and ceiling of the wine cellar. While time consuming, this is a fun finish to apply and looks remarkably like real stone.

Proper preparation of the walls was critical to ensure the finish would wear well over the years. The basement smelled dank, so we washed the walls with a bleach wash to destroy any possible mildew. The basement is two- thirds underground, so a certain amount of moisture naturally permeates through the cement block walls. To prevent this, we used Dry-loc™ moisture sealing paint mixed with an anti-mildew paint additive. We also added Paint Pourri™ by Scentco to freshen the room. It comes in many scents and lasts up to six months. We chose a soft vanilla scent.

Adrienne troweled on 7 layers to achieve this pitted stone look

The pitted stone look is accomplished in slowly building up layers. First, the wall was primed with Texture Coat™. Once dry, SandStone™ was applied over 100% of the surface, followed by PlasterTex™ in continental shapes over approximately a third of the wall. Adrienne mixed 5 custom colors Old World Veneziano™: yellow ochre, gray, earth red and a golden sienna. She applied these in several layers building slowly and blending. She left some areas open and caught only the raised sandy areas to form the "pits". Once completed, Adrienne glazed the entire wall in earth brown to tone and tie together the colors. A final wax made of bowling alley wax mixed with Van Dyke Brown Aqua Color™ darkened the pitted areas. A final buff using a car waxer made the smooth areas shine for excellent contrast with the rough pitted areas.

Westover Winery sign represents the Westover neigborhood

This wall, painted by Susie Goldenberg of PAINTIN' THE TOWN FAUX, mimics an aged and weathered wine label sign. The name "Westover Winery" honors the quaint Westover neighborhood where the house is located.

It's not tile -It's troweled plaster over wood

Faux "tumbled marble" countertop: Wanda Timmons is famous for her inventive countertop finishes. This counter looked so much like real tumbled marble that a contractor admonished us for tiling over wood. When told it wasn't tile, he didn't believe us. Wanda primed the wood with Texture Coat™ followed by a layer of Sandstone™. Once dry, she taped off the grout lines with 1/4" tape. The Sandstone™ texture gives the faux "grout" realistic texture. For the "tile" Wanda used both Old World Marmarino™, Plastertex™ and Venetian Gem™ plaster and distressed with sea salt and putty knife. Each square was painted in varied shades of the colors of the wall and floor, then glazed and sealed.

Floor: Susie Goldenberg changed an ugly gray cement floor into this beautifully stained and "aged" floor using Bella Vernici Architectural Concrete Products®. She primed and stained the floor in colors to complement the walls. Susie applied a Modello Designs® floor pattern and used muratic acid to lift the stain. The result is a floor that looks one hundred years old and is perfect for a wine cellar.

Stairway to Wine Cellar

Embedded wine corks and labels, painted corks and wine glass all let visitors know they are entering a wine cellar

After

The gray steps were dry-walled on left side and woodgrained

Before

Artist Maggie O'Neill designed the basement stairwell around the wine cellar theme. She and her team embedded a variety of wine corks and labels into newly plastered walls, then aged the finish with an earth-toned glaze. A 3D niche at the top of the stairs includes a wine bottle she had cut in half.

Drywall was added to the left side of the steps and Maggie wood grained the both walls and stairs.

Just for fun Maggie painted two Trompe l'oeil corks and a broken wine glass on the stairs.

In progress

Maggie imbedded wine corks and labels into Versiplast™

Cork embedded in plaster

A trompe l'oeil cork on stair

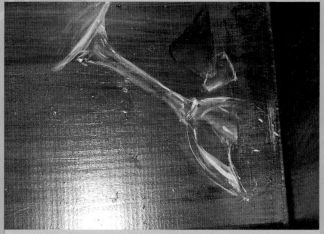

Broken wine glass painted on the stairs

Faux "stained glass"

Faux stained glass: was painted by muralist and faux finisher, Kate Nagle. She used acrylic simulated liquid leading to form the outline. Once dry, she applied Plaid Acrylic Gallery Glass™ paints in layers until she got the look she wanted. The faux stained glass serves to cover an ugly window, add a bit of color and reiterate the wine cellar theme.

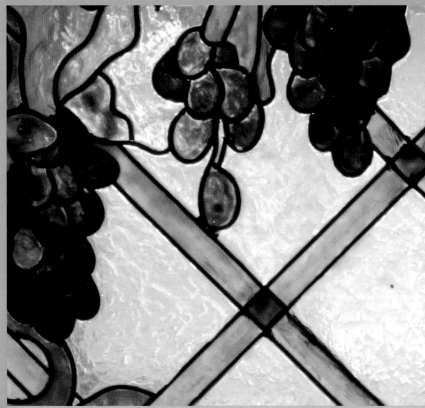

It's painted Plexiglas™!

Faux stone light: The mini-can lights seemed too modern for the old world feel of the room. Beaux-Artes sells decorative medallions to fit around lights and vents. We applied Pro Faux® Pro-Sandstone™ on the moldings and over the Westover sign for an old world stone look.

Inexpensive mural ordered on-line: It isn't necessary to spend a fortune to have a lovely mural. This paper mural was ordered and custom sized on-line from muralsyourway.com. Similar options include room size murals on wallpaper available through the Mural School and printed giclee murals on canvas may be purchased through Faux Effects® Inc., Vigini, and other studios.

"Stone" light

Inexpensive paper mural

Mural at the base of the stairwell

Painted note

Faux cabinet hides water turn-off

Mural painted with heat-set oils: by Mary Kingslan-Gabilisco was attached at the base of the stairs and creates the illusion of depth, making the wine cellar seem larger. Mary paints with Genesis Heat Set Oils®. These paints and your brushes will stay wet for months allowing time to work wet on wet. Conversely a painting can be finished in a day because each layer can be dried in minutes with a special heat gun or oven.

Room Captain Adrienne van Dooren and Room Lieutenant Celeste Stewart celebrate with a glass of wine

Artists:

Adrienne van Dooren - Room Captain, design, pitted stone & faux leather
Celeste Stewart - Room Lieutenant and wine racks
Susie Goldenberg - cement floor and wine label mural
Annie Lemarié - faux wood wine barrel
Kate Nagle - faux stained glass
Michael Gross - trompe l'oeil wine cabinet
Wanda Timmons - faux tumbled marble countertop
Mary Kingslan Gibilisco - trompe l'oeil mural
Rebecca Hotop - painted glass holder
Ann Bayer - staging
Team Members - Lisa Turner, Anne Bayer, Robin Bear, Hector Lopez, Rebecca Hotop, Tracie Weir, Debbie Dennis, Carol Patterson, & Mitch Eanes
Maggie O'Neill: Project Captain/Primary Artist basement stairwell
Stacy Matarese-Project Lieutenant - faux inlaid wood door
Team Member- Christine Barnette

Sponsors:

Arlington Paint and Decorating Center-painting supplies and acid
Beaux- Artes-decorative moldings
Bella Vernici Architectural Concrete™-cement overlay stain products
Color wheel- Versiplast
Dominion Floors-sealing stairs
Faux Effects® International-plasters, texture products & tools
Faux Fingers™-trowels
Faux Like a Pro®-wax
Genesis Heat Set Oils™-used in trompe l'oeil mural
Kelly S. King-invented pitted stone and aged leather finishes
Kingslan-Gabilisco Studios-heat set oils
Krylon®-plastic primer
Murals your way™-wine country mural inside arch
Nash Timber Corp. -plastic industrial barrel
Paintin The Town Faux-Westover mural and floor products
Pro Faux®-sandstone used on moldings
Rockland Industries - Roc-lon Multi-purpose cloth for arch mural
The Mad Stencilist Embellishments Say What? - "say what" stencil
Modello Designs™-decorative masking pattern for concrete floor design
Scentco™-vanilla scented paint additive
Stencil Planet-stencil for faux inlaid wood door
Steve Brown Construction-light installation

63

Before

6' - 6" ceiling and no windows

After

Black ceiling and panels make room look bigger

What we did:

- Painted cement floor
- Painted ceiling black
- Wood grained drywall
- Added faux leather panels
- Installed ventless gas fireplace
- Painted trompe l'oeil "molding"
- Painted grouse and faux frame
- Wood grained doors to resemble inlay
- Bordered panels with upholstery tacks
- Added door escutcheon and decorative vent
- Replaced overhead lights with up-lighting

Gentleman's Room

The Gentleman's Quarters is intended to be a place where a man can feel at home – to relax by a fire with a cognac and cigar

Artist Julie Miles, Tania Seabock, and Brad Duerson took a basement room that was small and claustrophobic and turned it into the favorite room in the house. The room was long and narrow and had extremely low ceilings (6'6"). The white walls, narrow dimensions and lack of any windows made it dark and uninviting.

Julie applied several decorating tricks to make the room appear much larger. Surprisingly, painting the ceiling black made it visually disappear. Replacing ceiling can lights with sconces which provided up lighting rather than down lighting also made the ceiling appear taller. They also painted the majority of the wood grain vertical rather than horizontal so that the eye is led upward. Another secret to making small rooms appear larger is to maintain a singular color palette. In this case, the floor, furniture and walls are in varied hues of brown. This not only visually enlarges the space, it also creates a sense of comfort and calm. One myth about decorating small rooms is that one should use miniaturized furniture. In some cases, using fewer large pieces actually enhances the visual flow.

To make the narrow room seem wider, Julie and Tania broke up the long expanse of white walls by adding panels and a chair rail. The panels also compensated for the lack of windows. The drywall was wood grained by Julie and Tania to resemble rich walnut. Tania added trompe l'oeil molding which fooled even the photographer. The upper panels were given the look of faux aged leather using lincrusta with hand painted details, then finished with a patina glaze. Upholstery nail strips were used to set the panels apart from the faux wood.

The transformation was dramatic. The room now feels lighter, the ceilings higher and visitors want to sit and stay a while, proving once again that life is too short for white walls and ceilings!

Faux leather is painted lincrusta and upholstery tacks

Grouse and "frame" are painted

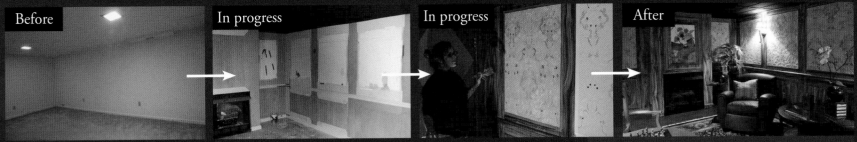

Before · In progress · In progress · After

The ceiling was painted black, then wooden strips added because originally, the team planned to attach antiqued mirrors. However, after hanging several they discovered the mirrors made the ceiling feel lower and too modern for the room. So the mirrors were removed but the gridwork remained. Brad decided to leave the ceiling black, a surprisingly effective look. The harsh overhead lights were replaced with eight sconces purchased at Home Depot for just $50 each. These lights add an elegant touch, make the ceiling appear higher and the room cozier. They also add visual depth to the walls of panels.

The antique leather look within each panel was accomplished by purchasing lincrusta, a white paper & plaster product available in many styles and designs. Since the lincrusta is white, Julie and her team first basecoated, then enhanced the details with subtle color. Once dry, the process was completed with a chalky patina glaze.

The wood graining was accomplished in 3 steps, a basecoat of straw yellow, an acrylic layer flogged with a specialty brush and a final painted layer. Tape was used to create the faux joints and the wood grained in the proper direction for each "piece of wood".

"Wood molding" is _painted_ on drywall

Photo by Omar Salinas

Trompe l'oeil details painted by Tania Seabock to give the illusion of true 3-D moldings.

Artists & Sponsors

Artists:

Julie Miles and Brad Duerson - Room Captains
Tania Seabock - Artistic Designer /wood-grained trompe l'oeil moldings
Mau-Don Nuyen and Nancy AtLee - Furnishings/Decor
Team Members - Stuart Kershner, Hector Lopez, Ian Seabock, Celeste Stewart, Ann Bayer, Linda O'Neill, Barb Tise, Lisa Turner, Tracy Weir, Ceil Glembocki and Carol Patterson

Sponsors:

Arlington Paints and Decorating - paint and supplies
Beaux-Artes - Decorative vents and door escutcheon
Curtain, Upholstery and Furniture, LLC - furniture
Golden Artists Colors Inc. - acrylic paint
Hand-made carpet in India by Sphinx/Oriental Weavers
Oriental Rugs and More - Leesburg VA Corner Outlets

Before

After

Basement laundry is converted to a bathroom

68

Trompe l'oeil woman "caught" in just her towel

What we did:

- *Finished basement bath*
- *Replaced cement sink and moved washer / dryer*
- *Wood grained doors and trim*
- *Added clear glass shower*
- *Applied same plaster on floors, walls and ceiling*
- *Created Venetian plaster faux fresco murals*
- *Trompe l'oeil woman in towel surprises visitors*
- *Painted PVC pipe like bronze*
- *Added low water modern toilet*

Basement Bathroom

A tiny basement laundry is now a much needed 2nd bath

Jne' Medellin, created a Greek bath using her unique method of painting with Behr® Venetian plaster. She used tiny faux fingers® trowels to apply the plaster, much as artists use pallet knives with textured oil paints. Jne' used Modello® adhesive stencils for the basic outline of the Grecian women and urns and did the rest by hand, carefully layering on color, light and shadow.

Jne' completed the murals in her studio on Roc-lon™ cloth and attached them on-site. By blending the same color background plaster from each panel out to the walls, she was able to hide the canvas edges. The panels resemble fresco. Jne' also covered the ceiling and floor in the same plaster for a seamless finish. The floor was then finished with several layers of sealer.

The bath was already plumbed but had never been finished as a bath. It primarily held the washer, dryer and a long cement sink. Reconfigured for convenience and function it is now a much needed second bath.

Venetian Plaster Mural

The area seemed too small for a full bath and had 6'6" ceilings with pipes running along portions of the ceiling. We had the ceiling dry-walled and finished in the same color as the walls. Most important, Jne' chose a frame-less glass shower. Almost invisible, it makes the room look more open. Similarly, the glass sink is clear and takes up far less room than a traditional sink. Having the faucet extend from the wall is also a space-saver. The glass, reflective plaster, low profile toilet, mural of the open door, and monochromatic color-scheme all serve to enlarge an incredibly tiny yet beautiful space.

The faux fresco murals and urns in this stunning bathroom invoke a sense of peace and tranquility.

They also make an elegant statement usually reserved for palaces and grand hotels.

Artists:
Jne' Medellin - Room Captain/walls
Elizabeth T. Lee - Room Lt/Venetian plaster floor
Machyar Gleuenta - mural of woman in doorway
Team Members - Celeste Stewart and Mitch Eanes

Sponsors:
Behr® - Venetian plaster
Faux Effects® International - basecoat and bronze metalics, and sealers for floor
Faux Fingers™ - miniature trowels
Noland Plumbing - sink and fixtures
Modello Designs® - decorative masking pattern
Roc-lon™ - canvas

Tissue paper finish / raised   **Medallion stencil on wood floor**

Closets and small baths need not be boring. In fact, this is where you can go wild with color, texture and design. Since this hall closet is located just outside the romantic bedroom, Carol chose a romantic theme and brought in the pale blue. She added lots of texture and pearlecsent accents for interest and a stenciled element for fun.

What we did:

- *Stenciled a hat box, shoes and mannequin just for fun*
- *Applied raised stenciled angels to walls*
- *Glued crumpled tissue paper over 100% of wall*
- *Basecoated walls in pearlecent white*
- *Put stencils back over designs and painted with irridescents*
- *Painted floor medallion using a Jan Dressler adhesive stencil*
- *Painted door panels silver, then troweled denim Lusterstone™ through a floral patterned lace to resemble needlepoint*

Small Space
Left Hall Closet
by Lisa Turner

Imprinted fern **Shimerstone™ & Orastone™**

This hall closet just outside the "stone" bath was the perfect place to demonstrate the beauty of texture. Lisa created a stone look with fern "fossils" yet, as a fun surprise the walls have a slight metallic glow

What we did:
- *Troweled metallic plasters on the door*
- *Applied plaster to the interior walls*
- *Pressed rubber fern stamps into wet plaster*
- *Glazed walls in warm earth tones*
- *Displayed birdhouses to be auctioned for Noah's Wish*

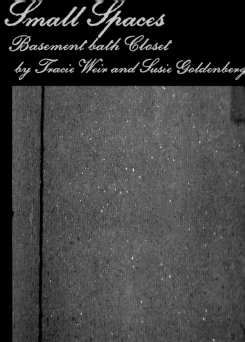

Parvati Textured Cotton ▶
Plaster with gold, pearl and
silver filaments feels as good
as it looks. The sea shells
Tracie Weir glued to the ceiling have similar pink tones.

Parvati™ Textured Cotton

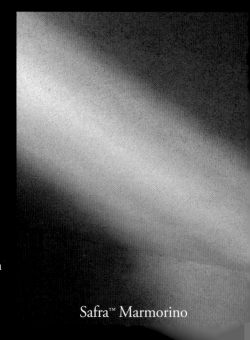

Safra™ Marmarino lime ▶
based plaster was applied by Ian
Seabock for the School of Italian Plasters. It provides a rich
natural look to the rear wall.

Safra™ Marmorino

Small Space
Main Floor Half Bath
by Shawn Bessenyei

Oikos Venetian Plaster

This close-up shows the beauty of Venetian plaster. To obtain this effect, 3-5 layers of plaster are tightly troweled and burnished to a shine. The walls appear to have texture and depth yet are smooth to the touch.

Shawn Bessenyei transformed the tiny white half bath by adding color and texture. He cut an arch in drywall and attached it on top of the existing plaster. He finished the arches in red Venetian plaster and the inset area and ceiling in an earth toned Oikos lime plaster. He also replaced the sink with a corner model to open up the space.

Artists
Shawn Bessenyei - Half bath
Lisa Turner - Upper hall "fern" closet
Carol Patterson - upper hall "tissue paper" closet
Tracie Weir - downstairs bath
Josh Yavelberg - closet surprise mural
Susie Goldenberg - Parvati Texture Cotton Plaster
Ian Seabock-plaster, downstairs bath

Sponsors
Andreae Stencils - trowels and tools
Behr® - Pearlescent paint
Color Wheel - Modern Masters paints and Oikos plasters
Faux Effects® International - tissue paper, Aquastone™, Lusterstone™ and Irridecent Venetian Gem™ Highlight™ colors
Golden Artists Colors Inc®.- Irredecent colors
Jan Dressler - stencils for shoes, mannequin & adhesive vinyl floor design
Plaza Artes - metalics
Paintin the Town Faux - Parvati Texture
Stencil Planet - Angel Stencils
School of Italian Plasters - Safra™ marmarino

Finishes
Kelly King - teaches the imbedded fern finish and plaster and lace
Melanie Royals - teaches raised stencil under tissue paper
School of Italian Plasters - teaches marmarino application
Paintin the Town Faux - teaches Parvati application

Before

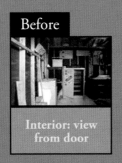

Before

Interior: same angle as opposite page

Interior: view from door

Old Shed Becomes Home Office
Elegant yet whimsical,
this room tells a story...

Exterior was an eyesore

Volunteers primed shed

Needs decorative accents

The Faux House was too small to include a home office, a near necessity in today's world. The only other space available was an old storage shed. Room Captain Mary Steingesser decided to convert the exterior shed into an office with a botanical artist's theme.

It appears this mischievous pig broke through the opposite wall and is now wrapped in wallpaper

Photo by Omar Salinas

What we did:

- *Painted exterior/added decorative accents*
- *Added insulation, drywall, and small heater*
- *Attached canvas murals*
- *Faux painted walls and ceiling*
- *Added window treatments*
- *Applied Skimstone™ over gray cement floor*
- *Stenciled floor design with tinted cement*
- *Created custom molds for ceiling design*
- *Revived old furniture found in shed*

Painted window visually opens the room

Even non-artists can create these whimsical animals. Both the donkey left and the pig on the facing page were painted using stencils by The Mad Stencilist™. They were then hand embellished with details and added shadows. The window illusion was made even more convincing by adding real molding and curtains for a third dimension.

Floral painting by Mary Steingesser
Mary painted six acrylic on gold botanicals to further illustrate the room's theme.

Sheri Hoeger painted a trompe l'oeil "paneled" door with hanging overalls. She used an airbrush to shade the overalls which are paint-spattered in keeping with the artist's studio theme. Sheri completed the canvas in California and shipped it to Virginia where volunteers used wallpaper adhesive to attach it to the existing flat wooden door. The before photo (right) shows how this simple change adds tons of character to the room.

76

After

Painted door molding & Overalls on flat door

Before

Flat wood door

After

Custom molded ceiling design

Ceiling: The ceiling was fauxed along with the walls, then Mary created this one-of-a-kind ceiling medallion made of hand-cast plaster. The design complements the floor design and adds elegance to the room.

After

Floor: Skimstone™ is a cement overlay product that can be easily applied by the DIYer using a how-to DVD. Volunteers mixed a pale green shade and troweled it over the existing gray cement floor. To make the design, they used a Modello® stencil and darker varied colors of Skimstone™.

Skimstone was troweled over gray cement floor

Before

After

Old Army desk updated with paint & plaster

This metal cabinet was found in the shed and given new life

Before

After

Applying Wood Icing™ to furniture is a fun and easy process

Raised stenciled design in Venetian plaster

78

After

hinge strap

door escutcheon ornaments

faux shutters

Faux dog

Painted shutters, window boxes and other details change the shed from eyesore to cozy cottage

Before

Painted slats for "shutters"

Ashley Spencer added butterflies to symbolize the rebirth of her home town, New Orleans

Birdhouses

Photo by Omar Salinas

Artists:
Mary Steingesser - Room Captain
Linda O'Neill - Room Lieutenant
Sheri Hoeger - painted overalls door panel
Rose Wilde - Wood Icing™ cabinet makeover
Francesca Springolo: donkey in window
Anne Bayer - Army desk makeover
Ceil Glembocki - window treatments, dog pillow and flowers
Ashley Spencer - trompe l'oeil shutters and butterflies
Denise Malueg - pig in torn paper
Debbie Thompson - matting and framing
Gary Arvanitopulos - concrete step with dog prints
Chris Jackson - flowers in window boxes
Celeste Stewart - exterior woodwork
Stuart Kershner - decorative moldings
Sally Skene - landscape for large mural
Team Members - Lee Hickman, Ryoko Kanke, Kathy Keel,
Linda Manning, Carol Rohrbaugh, Jacky Shaw, Sally Skene,
Jenny Vanier-Walker, Eric of Paintin the town Faux, Carl Bayer,
Rachel Steingesser, Tracie Wier, Barb Tise, Marc Steingesser,
Jennifer Skene, Tania Seabock, Ann Cook, Eric Carleton, Susan
Guarino, and Patrick O'Neill

Sponsors:
Andreae Stencils™ - stencils
ArtStuf™ - molding supplies
Beaux-Artes - door escutcheon and hinge straps
Calico Corners® - fabric for window treatments
Color Wheel - Skimstone™
Faux Effects International-paints and glazes for walls
Golden Artists Colors®, Inc.-paint
Hanging Treasures - custom picture frames
Keepmypet.com™ - preserved dog
Mad Stencilist™ - donkey pig and floral stencils
Modello Designs® - decorative masking floor pattern
Roc-lon® - canvas for murals
SALI - Capital Area Decorative Painters-volunteers
Skimstone™ - cement floor products
Stencil Planet™ - stencils
Wood Icing™ - rejuvenated cabinet

79

Before

After

Same door-woodgrained

Steps painted in faux brick

Painted faux "brick"

Photo by Omar Salinas

Exterior

The front entrance provides the first impression of a home. Unfortunately, the Faux House entrance screamed "dated". Just a few simple changes made a big difference.

Before

The most dramatic change came from the faux brick treatment by DC Concrete Technologies. They taped off and sprayed the finish right over the existing concrete walk. The color attracts the eye from the street to the front door.

What we did:
- Updated landscaping
- Replaced light fixture
- Removed metal awnings
- Wood grained front door
- Painted gray shutters black
- Replaced wooden rails with iron
- Painted cement walk to look like brick
- Added decorative ornamentation above the door

81

Before

Ugly side entrance

Wood railing

Wood deck

Concrete Stoop

In progress

Side entrance was half wood deck and half concrete; a cement makeover and black wood stain bring the 2 together

The kitchen entrance: The landing was half wooden deck with a wood rail and half concrete stoop with an iron rail. This presented quite a design challenge. Cement specialist Dan Mahlmann decided to create faux wood from cement to tie the two materials together. He and Gary Arvanitopulos used cement overlay products and tints to create the look and texture of wood, right down to the grain, knots and joints. Within this faux wood frame, they created a faux stone inlay with a "carved" medallion. This look was accomplished by using a Modello® vinyl adhesive design over the first black layer and then applying the lighter layer of cement over it. Once the Modello® was pulled out, the image is engraved into the stone. The steps now resemble black stone with intricate detais such as real mica flakes. The wooden deck was stained in black to further blend the two spaces.

Cement looks and feels engraved

Before

After

After

Cement looks like wood

Cement overlay turns ugly porch into focal point

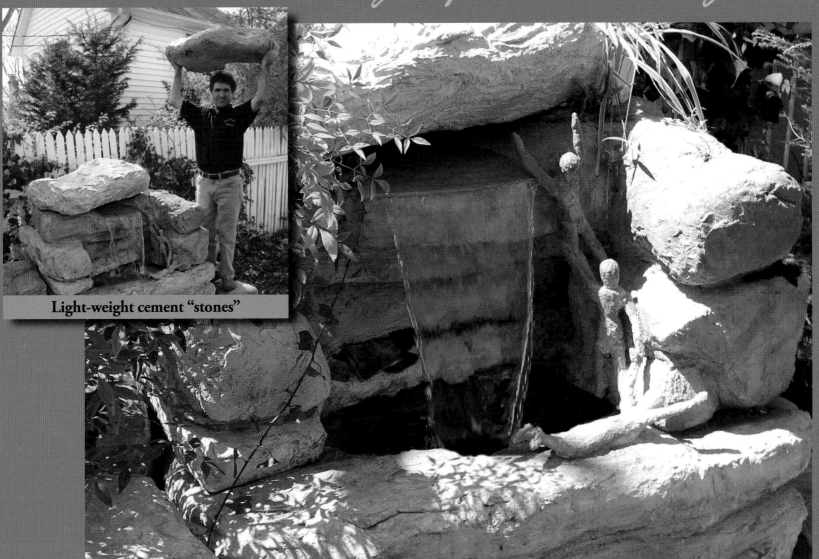

Light-weight cement "stones"

Fountain represents people of New Orleans helping each other escape the water and rubble

Gary Arvanitopulos of PA created this one-of-a-kind fountain out of lightweight materials covered in concrete. The "stone" is incredibly realistic. Gary used color variations copied from real stone and pressed in an occasional shell impression for a fossil look. The fountain represents New Orleans, with the people helping one another to rise out of the water and rubble of the hurricane to reach toward the sky of a new tomorrow. The calming sound of the waterfall makes the back yard a true oasis from a hectic world.

Before

In progress

After

After

Side door gets trim, mural and painted panels

Flower pot cut in half

The side entrance was truly an eyesore with its metal awning and rusty storm door. We removed the awning and storm door and added wood trim. Carolyn Blahosky painted a lovely country scene on canvas panel in her studio and later glued in into the door panel. She also stenciled the door and created wooden flower panels to hide the open storage area under the porch. The half flower pot, left covers an unsightly outlet, while the screen below hides the AC unit.

Wine bottle sculpture

Painted gourd birdhouses

Birdhouse screen hides AC unit

Before

After
Photo by Omar Salinas

Landscaping, stone path, and painted shed transform yard

Before

After
Photo by Omar Salinas

The house really had no landscaping to speak of. The grass met the walkway and driveway and the shed looked – well – like a shed, making the space seem utilitarian. Landscaper Chris Jackson created a private retreat by using shrubs and plants to form a boundary for the yard and separate it from the walk and gravel drive. His use of curves softened the existing harsh geometric shapes of the house, brick walk, and patio. Chris also added a stone path connecting the two brick patio areas. Finally, window boxes, patio pots and hanging plants added both color and character.

In the front, Chris removed and transplanted the overgrown bushes and replaced them with smaller azaleas and colorful phlox. Two tall holly bushes were chosen to frame the front steps. Chris then rounded the yard's strait lines for a softer more welcoming look.

After

Before

After

Boring to Beautiful with Simple Art: the patio was updated with just a few simple changes. Stuart Kershner applied a very thin foam insulation and wood panel to cover the bead board paneling. He then glued a Beaux-Artes molding piece top and bottom for a beautiful carved wood look. He added composite molding pieces to the upper 3 panels for balance. The addition of one of their specialty doorknob ornaments over the existing inexpensive knob makes the door very elegant indeed. Volunteers painted the windows to look etched.

Before

After

After

Rusty mailbox gets new look

Carol Farley of Maryland took on the challenge of making over the rusty, dented mailbox. She primed and painted the mailbox a cheerful blue, then attached mirrors and broken ceramics for a fun mosaic pattern complete with house numbers. She also added whimsical flowers, teacup handles, and even a little bird to tie in with our birdhouse theme.

Artists:

Celeste Stewart - Project Captain
Chris Jackson - Landscaper
Gary Arvanitopulos - Ode to New Orleans fountain and porch
Ann and Carl Bayer - birdhouse screen and open house signs
Carolyn Blahosky - side entrance artwork
Carol Farley - mailbox
Stuart Kershner - decorative moldings
Suzanne Leedy - photos and bottle sculpture
Dan Mahlmann - concrete side porch and shed entrance
Dennis Nash - side entrance molding
Ashley Spencer - trompe l'oeil shutters
Barb Tise - color consultant
DC Concrete technologies team - Justin Velez-Hagan, Russell Sellineer, Reginald Fleming, Lewis Lewis, Skip Calvert and Dorothy Schmitt

Sponsors:

Action Iron - iron railings
Arlington Paints and Decorating Center - paints and brushes
Benjamin Moore® - exterior paints and primers
Beaux-Artes - decorative moldings, hinge ornaments and door-knob escutcheon
Chris Jackson Landscaping - landscape design & labor
Andrea Stencils - birdhouse stencils for screen
Color Alchemist School and Restoration - exterior painting
Colesville Nursery - holly plants
DC Concrete Technology - front entrance concrete
Decorative Concrete of Maryland, Inc. - side entrance
Decorator's Supply - composite moldings
Faux Effects® International - mica flakes and stain
Golden Paints Artists Colors Inc.√ - painted planters and paint
Home Depot® - exterior lighting

Krylon Paints® - primers and black paint for iron rails
Modello Designs® - decorative masking pattern
Royal Design Studio® - side window stencils
Stencilworks - stencils, wooden panels and painted table
Mad Stencilist - stencils for the exterior of the shed
Priscilla Hauser - birdhouse idea books
Pure Texture Concrete - fountain materials
Red Lion Stencils - stencils
Restoration Hardware√ - fire pit
Roc-Lon® - canvas
Thompson Creek Windows - windows and copper for bay window
Wing Enterprises® - Little Giant Ladder™

The Chicago Project: Church of the Atonement

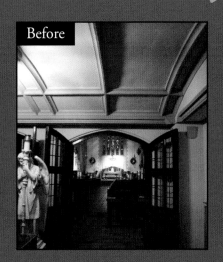

Before

When the House that Faux Built Project became too large for the Arlington House, this intercity Chicago church and rectory provided an excellent pallet for the additional artisans. The church and rectory had beautiful lines and architectural elements, but over the years they had either deteriorated or had simply been painted white.

What we did:

• Created and donated Icon

• Fauxed the church's main hallway

• Added art/faux to 3 rooms of the rectory

• Painted and gilded Narthex ceiling and walls

• Attached ceiling mural and fauxed ceiling in hall

• Added mural and floor cloth to women's rest room

• Planned fresco for the sanctuary to begin spring 2007

Before

Before

In progress

Narthex ceiling went from white cement to WOW!

The Narthex
by Jacek Prowinski

Jacek painted the white cinder-block walls to look like stone

Artist Jacek Prowinski is renowned throughout the United States for his church preservation and restorations. To ensure this project stayed true to the original style, he carefully researched the church archives. Jacek was determined to provide the parishioners a sense of all that had been in the hearts and minds of those first families who met together to establish such a wonderful church.

The Narthex is the entrance to the church, but white cinder-block walls and a gray cement ceiling were anything but inviting. Jacek remedied this by painting the walls in earth tones to replicate stone blocks and adding color to the ceiling. The ceiling was in disrepair so Jacek applied lime-based plaster to smooth the concrete. He then hand-painted each panel with a historical floral pattern and gilded the moldings. He added English crosses over silver-leafed shield backgrounds to add dimension and reflect the character of the church.

After

After

This entry leading to the fellowship hall was not in the original faux plan. However, Chicago artists Chesna Koch and Sue Sidun felt the entrance would be the perfect place to hang the domed ceiling Giclee by Yves Lantheir. Once hung, it was apparent the ceiling needed glazing and aging... which of course made the wall and upper molding look too white. So we glazed the walls in a slightly lighter version of the ceiling color making the cinder block resemble stone block. The ugly bulletin board didn't fit in with this new look, so Adrienne painted it black and attached Beaux-Artes moldings to make it look more like art. All of this was done in just one day!

The Church Entrance and Hallway

Icon by Tania Seabock using traditional methods

Visitors of all faiths are welcome to attend church to see the artwork in this chapter:

The Church of the Atonement
5749 North Kenmore Avenue
Chicago, IL 60660
Phone: 773-271-2727
Fax: 773-271-4295
info@ChurchOfTheAtonement.org
www.ChurchOfTheAtonement.org

Printed canvases are a cost effective way for homeowners to add beautiful art to their walls and ceilings. Heavier canvases require construction adhesive. It is important to have several people to apply the canvas because it must be held in place until set. It is also possible to hire a wall paper professional.

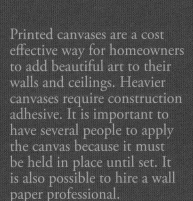

Giclee mural by Yves Lanthier

Artists:

Jacek Prowinski - Narthex
Team members: Maciej Adamek, Maros Koncok, Miroslav Sebestik
Chesna Koch-ceiling, molding church hallway
Jeff Ingram and Brian Townsend - giclee mural
Yves Lanthier - giclee ceiling mural
Leonard Pardon - faux marble floor cloth
Paulette Piaza - walls church entrance
Tania Seabock - Icon
Sue Sidun-church entranceway ceiling
Adrienne van Dooren- church entranceway, walls & bullitin board

Sponsors:

Beaux-Artes - Moldings
Faux Design Studio-Chicago
Roc-lon cloth - Floorcloth canvas
The Mad Stencilist - Mounting wax and Daige Waxer
Faux Effects® International
Easy Leaf
Zinsser products

After

Before

Church of the Atonement
Rectory Dining Room

by Gary Lord

Boring panels come alive with metallic foil finish

What we did:

• *Gave monochromatic panels pizzazz*

• *Applied metallic foils in four pastel colors*

• *Troweled Lusterstone® through lace*

• *Gilded the trim*

• *Applied glazes under the chair rail*

Kathy Carroll and her class assisted Gary with this beautiful finish. From left to right: Joanne Voll, Simona Grigorjevaite, Jenna DeFalco, Gary Lord, Kathy Carroll and Michele Cady.

At the completion of the Chicago Project all artists and volunteers were invited for a celebration and tour. Shown here are Adrienne van Dooren, Sheri Hoeger & Melanie Royals

The Rectory's large formal dining room is used 2-3 times a week for church dinners, meetings and entertaining. The large wall panels had been painted with contrasting trim but were simply lost on the wall.

Gary Lord, author of *It's Faux Easy*, used his signature foil sheets and lace to create these beautiful glimmering panels. Assisted by Kathy Carroll and her students from the Chicago Institute of Fine Finishes, Gary applied multicolored foils of pale blue, pink, silver and gold. To create the floral pattern, he selected a lace that complemented the room's elegant décor. He then taped up the lace and troweled Lusterstone™ thru it. The lace can be washed, air dried and reused several times. The finished lace design resembles needlepoint. Below the chair rail, Kathy and her team applied Perfetto™ Glaze with colorants. The mouldings were painted with Blue Pearl™ Metallic Paint and aged with Blue Pearl™ Faux Colorant Umber.

Study

by Paulette Piaza and
Adrienne van Dooren

What we did:

- Wall:
  - Added an "antique map" as focal point
  - Applied Giclee map by Yves Lanthier
  - Troweled plaster over parts of the map
  - Glazed and aged the map and panel

- Bar:
  - Fauxed a laminate bar to look like snakeskin
  - Pulled cheesecloth into unusual patterns
  - Troweled plaster through the cheese cloth
  - Applied antique cherry stain
  - Rubbed on a darkened wax

Before

Kid's Room: An extra bedroom in the rectory was changed into a child's guest room for little god-daughter Anna, who frequently visits from Washington, D.C. The Williamsburg gray walls were far too solemn for a 3-year-old, and the small child's bed seemed lost under the high paneled walls. Artist Paulette Piazza of Denver is an accomplished mural artist, but she loved the ease and speed of the princess stage drape transfer by Elephants on the Wall. This paint by the numbers mural is so easy even the "artistically impaired" can do it. Each kit comes with the full size pattern, transfer/ carbon paper, instructions and a color guide. Paulette deviated from the list of recommended colors to match the colors in the bedspread. She also painted the trim work in these colors. One doesn't have to be a child to feel like a princess in this room!

What we did:

- Created a fun and feminine kid's room
  - Selected paint colors from the bedspread
  - Painted walls white and the trim in pastels
  - Painted a princess drape over the bed
- Added jungle animals to the adjoining bath

After

Kid's Room
by Paulette Piazza

Dancing Dinos Mural

The bath came to life when we added these darling animals, also completed from *Elephants on the Wall* transfers. The animals were painted by Kacki Berri and Emily Cato in Washington DC on Roc-lon cloth. Paulette and Adrienne then simply cut them out and pasted them on the wall for a whole new look. Once Anna outgrows the design, the animals can be easily removed. Dancing Dinos, above was painted by Allison Parker.

Before

Artists:

Gary Lord - Dining Room
Paulette Piazza - Kid's Room and Study
Emily Cato and Kacki Berry - Kids animals for bath
Adrienne van Dooren - Snakeskin Bar and Stairwell
Nicola Vigini - Grotesca panels for stairwell
Yves Lanthier - Canvas panel-study
Allison Parker- Dancing Dinos (pattern donated for Habitat)
Patti Newton - Designed the Elephants on the Wall transfers
Team Members - Chesna Koch, Sue Sidun, Kathy Carroll, Jenna DeFalco, Simona Grigorjevaite, Joanne Voll, and Michele Cady

Sponsors:

Elephants on the Wall - kids' room wall murals
Faux Effects® International - Lusterstone™
Golden Artists Colors Inc.® - acrylic paints
Prismatic Studios - metallic foils
Pro Faux - paint and glaze
The Faux School- glaze and materials
Roc-lon® - canvas

Jennifer Carrasco

William Cochran also does exterior trompe l'oeil as shown

Patricia Buzo and
Andreas Scholz

William Cochran

Len Garon

Adrienne van Dooren

Carol van Gerena

Murals, Floor Cloths & Furniture

Many artists wanted to participate in the House that Faux Built Project but could not travel. These artists generously donated murals on canvas and other items for display and auction.

Karen Derrico

Len Garon

Karen Derrico - Painting
Micheal Gross custom firescreen

Michel Nadai, France
Often teaches trompe l'oeil in the U.S.

Tania Seabock
Trompe l'oeil panel with painted tile and wood

Sean Crosby and Pierre Finkelstein
Painted at the International Salon of Artists

Pascal Amblard

Murals: For those that want a trompe l' oeil mural but can't paint, the landscape mural (lower left) is available as a reproduction in room sized wall-paper. Should you wish to learn to paint, Sean and Pascal started The Mural School in Deleware where they and others teach.

All the artists on this page have instructional DVDs. 10% of proceeds from those purchased through www.fauxhouse.com goes to Habitat for Humanity.

For novice painters, a portion of the proceeds for any paint by number transfers purchased through www. elephentsonthe wall giveback program also goes to habitat (you must specify The House that Faux Built as your charity of choice)

Acrylic
Seascape
Mural
by
Pascal
Amblard

Faux marble floor cloths by Leonard Pardon

The church has linoleum tile floors and, although they could have been etched and painted, it was not realistic in the time-frame we had. The church's hallway is highly frequented so restricting traffic for the days it would have taken to prep, paint, dry and seal was simply not realistic. Therefore floor cloths were the perfect solution. Floor cloths are an excellent way to cover an unsightly floor. If properly sealed, they can stand up to high traffic and frequent cleaning in areas such as a kitchen or porch. Best of all you can take them with you when you move, so they are great for military families and renters.

Randy Ingram and Brian Townsend

A donated mural by Randy Ingram and Brian Townsend is perfectly complemented by a painted "inlay marble" Floorcloth by Leonard Pardon. Together they transform a dingy bath in the Chicago church project.

Floor Cloth by Leonard Pardon
is depicted here in both the bath (top) and main church hallway (lower photo). This illustrates the versatility of such a design. The floorcloth adds both color and beauty to an otherwise drab hallway

Beaux- Artes Moldings
These pre-finished moldings were glued and nailed around the canvas to wall to make canvas panel look like a large framed painting. We used the same style molding to frame the bulletin board

Sherrie Hoeger
Floor Cloth using her Mad Stencilist design

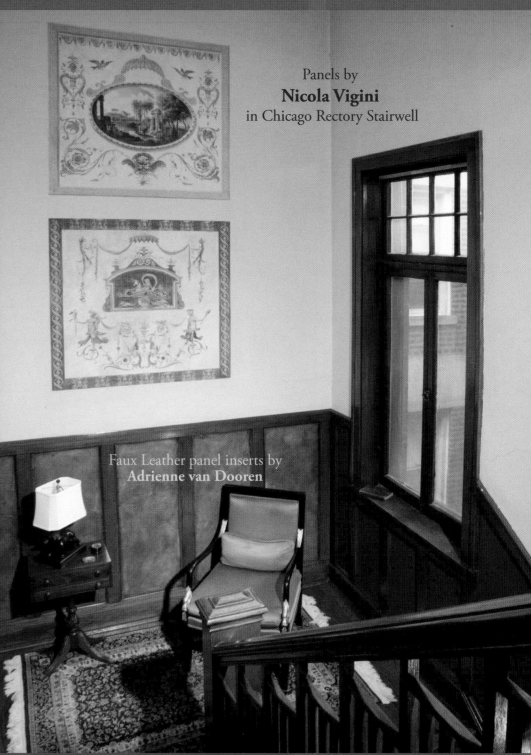

Panels by
Nicola Vigini
in Chicago Rectory Stairwell

Faux Leather panel inserts by
Adrienne van Dooren

Julie Miles
Floor Cloth using Modello® floor pattern

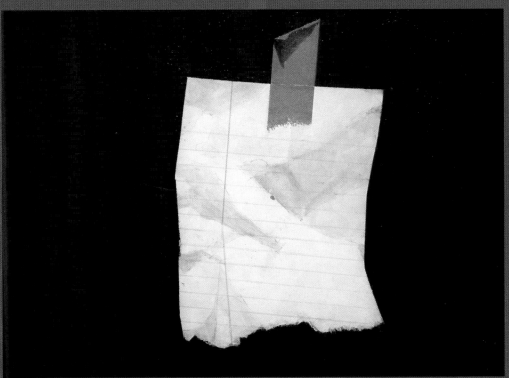

Adrienne van Dooren
Painted paper and tape on painted woodgrain

Paula Blackwell - textured mural

Melanie Kershner-mural in oils

Murals

Paulette Piazza
Sky mural in acrylic

iLia Anossov Modern Fresco

108

Photo by Suzanne Leedy   Photo by Suzanne Leedy

A wooden trash can was built by Michael Gross specifically to fit with the Italian theme of the Arlington kitchen. Michael used art transfers (Art Imprints™) made by Faux Effects® International, then aged and distressed it for an old world look. Patti Irwin used casein paints for this $10 yard sale table makeover for the Arlington kitchen.

Patti Irwin   **Patti Irwin**   **Shireen Balkissoon**   **Luba Marx**

An ordinary armoire was made to look elegant by attaching and gilding steam on composite molding. The scene within the circles was accomplished using colored pencils.

Kelly King teaches furniture make-overs in his Omaha studio.
He remade this old piece using crackle and gold leaf.

Furniture can be Repainted to Look Like Wood

Kathleen Sakry updated an old piece by painting it in a faux burl and adding trompe l' oeil molding and butterflies.

Wood graining:

Old Painted furniture, kitchen cabinets, book-shelves, etc need not need be stripped and refinished. While it takes practice and skill, painted furniture can be made to look like expensive wood or wood inlay. Move to a house with white painted cabinetry? Don't rip it out, repaint it to resemble cherry, walnut, pickled oak, etc.

Faux inlay wood by Laura Tust

Green table by Kathy Boyd has "insert" of faux wood

111

Have Fun with Furniture

Before

Patty Irwin adds fun to unfinished furniture

After

Traditionally Painted Furniture

Birdhouse lamp by Nancy *Petree* in keeping with our birdhouse theme

Side view

Close-up details of Rebecca's bird and floral design

Armoire by Rebecca Parsons features beautifully painted birds and flowers

Trompe l'oeil banana shipment chest by Jeff Monsein has a very realistic "hole" in the top

Refrigerator by Phillis Palmer and Jonie Fife

Sponsors:
Faux Effects® International
Golden Paints
Hanging Treasures
Johnie Liliandahl
Mad Stencilist
Modello Designs®
Roc-lon®

The contest called for any shape, any size, and this one by Kathi Ryan- Reagan was over four feet tall!

It was also representative of New Orleans from the ocean to the town and was made up of seven birdhouses.

Resident Mockingbird

A bird set up residence right outside the fauxhouse.

This New Orleans style art studio by Kerry Trout comes with its own miniature birdhouse

Why Birdhouses?

At the same time artists were working on the Faux House to raise money for *The Habitat House that Faux Built*, additional artists from around the world were busy with their own miniature faux houses to raise money for the feathered and furry animal victims of Katrina.

We were amazed and delighted at the talent, creativity and effort evident in each birdhouse. The winners and runners up of our contest are pictured on the next few pages.

The birdhouses were auctioned and the proceeds provided to Noah's Wish, a non-profit animal rescue organization. To learn more about this important charity go to www.noahswish.com

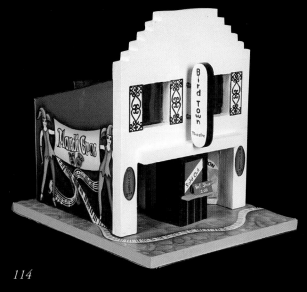

This birdhouse by Donna Busch of Canada was selected to be donated with the Habitat House that Faux Built so that both the people and animals get a home. The birdhouse is custom cut and painted to look like a New Orleans theater.

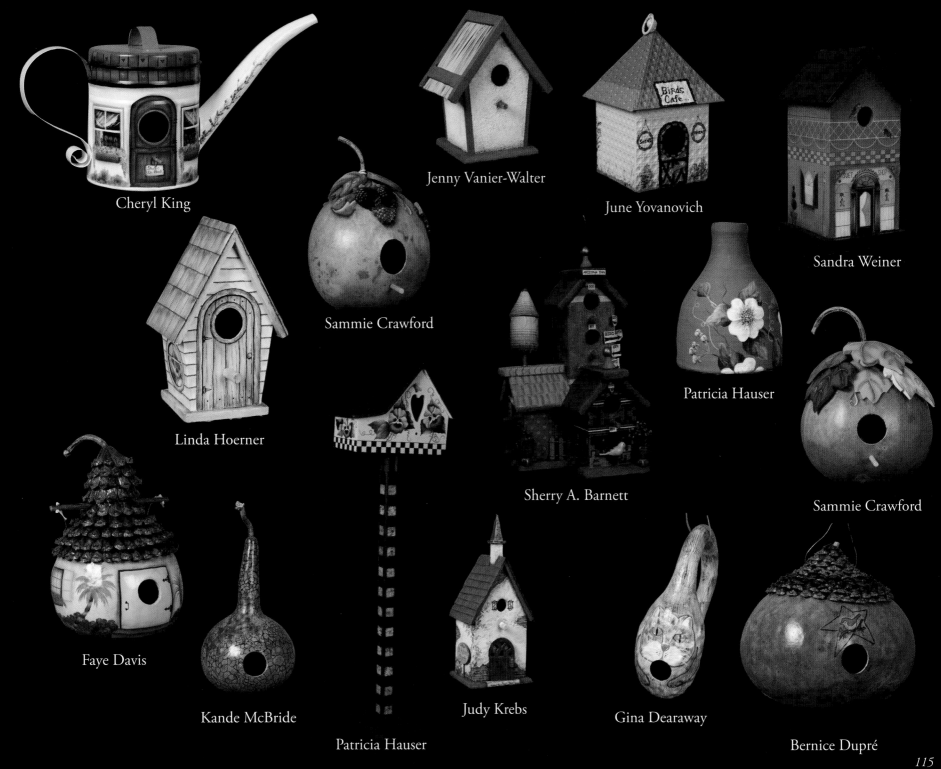

Cheryl King

Jenny Vanier-Walter

June Yovanovich

Sandra Weiner

Sammie Crawford

Linda Hoerner

Patricia Hauser

Sherry A. Barnett

Sammie Crawford

Faye Davis

Kande McBride

Judy Krebs

Gina Dearaway

Patricia Hauser

Bernice Dupré

Birdhouses

Kathryn Leonard

Audrey Nepper

Jonie Bassett

Cheri Perry

Terri M. Bayer

Joyce Moore

Becky Peterson

Kate Hill

Joyce Ann Clark

Judy Yett

Linda Kinnaman

Ann Bayer

Suzanne Leedy

116

Susan Rensch

Judy Luchino

Lorena M. Vicente

Carol Farley

Mary B. Walberg

Natini Kershav

Kathleen Hoegard

Debra Maerz

Debbie Brown

Annemairé Caola

Dorie Wilson

Judith A. MacLaren

Gina Dearaway

Louise Kramer

Jean Schettler

Laurin

117

Artists

Gary Arvanitopulos:
Born and raised in Greece, Argirios "Gary" Arvanitopulos has a natural talent in creating magnificent finishes. Owner of Exquisite Finishes located in Erie, PA, Gary boasts over 20 years of artistic experience. He began in jewelry fabrication and later expanded to faux finishes, including faux marbling, wood graining, gilding, glazing, old world finishes, fine furniture, and decorative concrete techniques. His combination of European and American training and culture makes his work unique. Known for his imagination and creativity, Argirios' work on the Arlington project includes the design and creation of the waterfall, the "engraved medallion," the shed entrance and concrete countertop in the kitchen.

www.exquisite-finishes.com

Pascal Amblard:
Pascal Amblard, France, specializes in trompe l'oeil and teaches internationally. His work has been exhibited in the largest international decoration show in Paris: Maison et Objet. Pascal is a co-owner and instructor at The Mural School, Deleware. He has several "how to" DVDs available at www.fauxhouse.com. Internationally known, Pascal has been invited to participate in the International SALON of Decorative Painting since 1998 and hosted it in 2001. His work has been displayed in many prestigious shows to include the Museum of Trompe l'oeil, Perigueux. Pascal contributed to the "Indian woman in the window" mural, Arlington project, and he created the seascape and landscape murals shown in the murals chapter.

www.themuralschool.com

www.pascalamblard.com/accueil.html

Ann Bayer
Ann Bayer, owner of Faux and Fleur Design Arlington, VA, partners with her husband, Carl to offer incredible decorative finishes for both residential and commercial clients. She has a studio display house which has the same layout as the Faux House. By appointment, potential customers and designers can actually see and touch many finishes on a variety of surfaces. She and Carl frequently travel the US for commissioned work. Due to Ann's superior finishing expertise and business sense, she was selected as Vice-Chair for Project Oversight and Hospitality. Ann also managed the open house events, fed and housed the majority of visiting artists, oversaw the budget, served as Room Captain for the living room, and painted the living room side table, old army desk, and decorative wooden birdhouse screen for the Arlington project.

FauxandFleur@aol.com

Paula Blackwell
An incredibly talented and creative faux finisher based in Portland Oregon, Paula Blackwell is well known for her skill, originality, and instructional skills. She is a top-notch decorative finisher and has completed many private mural and faux commissions across the U.S. Paula also shares her enthusiasm for her art by offering a variety of hands-on specialty classes. She further supports her passion for the industry and its continued growth by serving on the board of the Cascade Artisans Guild in Portland, Oregon. Paula is also an active member of the Stencilers Artisans League International and the North West Society of Interior Design. She completed the Nike texture painting featured in the murals and floorcloth chapter.

www.fauxdejour.com

Patricia Buzo
A professional mural artist, Patricia Buzo, has trained at some of the countries' finest art facilities. She began her journey when she was just 13 years old when she attended the Minnesota River School of Fine Art. Patricia later studied extensively in both formal educational settings and through intensive seminars and specialty workshops. Patricia's studio, known as Patricia's Pallet, specializes in decorative finishes such as fine faux effects and trompe l'oeil murals. A well known instructor, Patricia teaches trompe l'oeil, stenciling, and color theory classes. Patricia won WCCO Radio's "Good Neighbor Award" in July of 2004 and has appeared on HGTV's "Landscape Smart." Her beautiful donated landscape mural is featured in the mural and floorcloth chapter.

www.patricias-palette.com

Jennifer Carrasco
Jennifer Carrasco graduated with a BA in art and education from Washington State University and did graduate work at the University of Washington. In the 1960's, she worked as a Peace Corps Volunteer in the Philippines and remained in the country for 16 years, painting and teaching art. Jennifer has not only exhibited her fine art in galleries around the world, but has also become an established decorative painter, designing and executing everything from logos and illustrations for businesses, to trompe l'oeil residential and commercial murals. In 2005 Carrasco was chosen to create the Easter Egg poster for the White House. She is currently commissioned to create custom murals for Tommy Bahama stores in the US and abroad. Jennifer enjoys travel teaching and conducts regular seminars at Seattle Architectural Finishes Studio in Washington.

www.carrascomurals.com

William Cochran:
William Cochran has worked as a professional muralist for over twenty years. A trompe l'oeil master and teacher, most of his work is designed for American downtowns. Public Art Review called him "one of America's leading muralists." His immense attachment to the community shows in his touching street-scape work. Cochran's art has won numerous national awards, including the Project of the Year Award from the International Association for Public Participation (2001), the Project of the Year Award from the American Public Works Association (1999) for his Community Bridge, and the Award for Excellence from the American Glass Association. He has been called "a born teacher." His donated owl painting and an example of his amazing public art are found in the mural chapter.

www.WilliamCochran.com

Sean Crosby:
Sean Crosby is a self-taught artist with over 20 years experience. He began his professional career as a union bridge painter for the City of New York, and soon became the city's head instructor of painted decoration. Sean's projects have included the Russian Tea Room in New York City, the New York apartment of film stars Michael Douglas and Catherine Zeta-Jones, and the home of Hollywood director Michael Caton-Jones, His work has appeared in numerous highly-regarded national publications. Sean and Pascal Amblard own The Mural School in Delaware, one of the nation's highest regarded schools of mural, trompe l'oeil, graining, and marbling. Sean has several how-to DVDs available through our web site. He also is part of the four artist team who teach in Italy with Vigini studios. Sean contributed two mural panels to the project.

www.themuralschool.com

Karen Derrico:
Animals may not speak in real life, but for Karen Derrico they speak volumes on canvas. Using vivid colors and dimensional brush strokes in a semi-impressionistic style, her artwork is created exclusively with advanced digital painting tools. However, hers is anything but push-button artistry. Karen starts with a blank "canvas" and paints stroke by stroke to create her artwork, using photographs as a reference. Karen's talent for bringing animals to life through her art is gaining widespread recognition. As founder of Painting 4 Paws, she has raised more than $10,000 for animal charities. Karen donated the Westie painting and sleeping dog mural.

www.painting4paws.com

Deborah Drager:
Deb Drager owns Drager Design Studio and is the Director of Artimatrix Academy of Architectural Finishes, Wichita, KS. She is also a leading distributor of the Coral-liteTM products, as seen on the tub front of the HTFB master bath, Arlington project. Deb has a BFA in Fine Art and is a seasoned faux finisher, instructor, and graphic designer. Her original faux designs are regularly featured in several national magazines. Also proficient in graphic design, Deb was hired by Faux Effects® International to create marketing tools for the corporation, its network schools, and artisans. In addition to acting as Room Captain for the master bath, Deb assisted in designing this book.

www.ddrager.com

Brad Duerson:
Brad Duerson has a vast background of experience in historical restoration and building, including carpentry, tin-smithing (nearly a lost art), and masonry. He is also very accomplished at decorative painting, plasters, (e.g. Venetian, old world, and marmorino.) Brad served as Co-Room Captain for the Gentlemen's Room. He installed lighting, built in the fireplace, and assisted in the faux finishing. He also gave the male perspective on what should be included. www.jmilesstudios.com

Pierre Finkelstein:
Pierre Finkelstein is known internationally for his faux wood and marble techniques and tools. A published author and renowned instructor, he is a long-time member of Salon and a 1986 Gold Medal graduate of the Van Der Kellen Painting Institute in Brussels. Pierre was awarded "Best Craftsman In France" for decorative painting by the French Government in 1990. He is the owner of Grand Illusion Decorative Painting, Inc. and has created faux finishes for internationally acclaimed interior designers and architects. Pierre, along with Sean Crosby, Pascal Amblard,x and Nicola Vigini, completed the incredible Indian mural in the master bedroom.

www.pfinkelstein.com

Mary Kingslan Gibilisco:
Mary Kingslan Gibilisco, CDA, Omaha has had a lifelong interest in art. She began studying art formally in 1979 at the University of Nebraska and graduated Magna Cum Laude with a degree in Fine Art and a minor in Art History. In 1989, she received her Certified Decorative Artists distinction. She currently partners with her mother, Anne Kingslan, in their Omaha-based studio. Mary is a superior instructor on trompe l'oeil, realistic still lifes and the exciting new genesis heat-set oils. Her studio also carries a full line of instructional videos and booklets. Mary painted the trompe l'oeil mural for the base of the wine cellar steps, Arlington Project.

www.kingslan.com

Machyar Gleuenta:
Machyar Gleuenta was born and raised in Acheh, a northern region of Sumatra— the epicenter of the deadly earthquake and subsequent tsunami of December 26, 2004. He began his career in art working as an artist's helper in Acheh and later in Jakarta, Indonesia. His talents came to the attention of both the local and international communities and Machyar received a full scholarship from the Maine College of Art in Portland. Officials in the U.S. Embassy in Jakarta, as well as businessmen in Indonesia, helped raise the funds necessary for him to make his journey to America to begin his formal studies. Machyar also studied at the Pennsylvania Academy of Fine Arts in Philadelphia. MK painted the blond woman in towel in the basement bath.

www.mkfinearts.com

Susie Goldenberg:
Susie Goldenberg is the founder and director of Paintin' the Town Faux in Atlanta, Georgia. A Master Decorative Artist, she oversees client projects; operates her retail showroom and gallery; and teaches classes covering faux finishing, cabinet and furniture and concrete. Her work has been featured in decorative arts magazines, in many show houses throughout Atlanta, and HGTV. A Bella Vernici® distributor, she used the concrete overlay system and stains on the wine cellar floor. She also completed the Westover Winery sign and applied her signature Parvati Textures Cotton Plaster™ product in the master bath closet.

www.paintinthetown.com

Adrian Greenfield:
Adrian flew from Essex, England to participate in the House that Faux Built project. He originally trained as a painter but later discovered his passion was decorative art and murals. He now has over 10 years experience painting trompe l'oeil and murals, stenciling, and an extensive line of wall finishes. His works include a number of hotels, restaurants and private clients in Europe and in the US. He has been invited to participate in the International Artist Exchange 2007. Adrian's trompe l'oeil fireplace panel featuring realistic Dutch tile and his faux molding above the fireplace are featured in the Arlington project's Romantic Bedroom.

agelin@tiscali.co.uk

Sheri Hoeger:
Sheri Hoeger, better known as the "Mad Stencilist" of Placerville, CA, is nationally known for her airbrush stenciling techniques. Sheri offers workshops at her studio, the National SALI Convention, and premiere schools across the country. She also has a full line of stencils as well as the "Say What?TM" custom cut lettering system. Her product line includes the specialty wax and applicator tool used to apply murals in the HTFB. Sheri has been featured in several books, TV, and magazines. She painted the trompe l'oeil painter's overalls door panel for the Shed turned Artist's Studio. She also donated a floor cloth, stencils, and the Say WhatTM lettering for the upper hallway.

www.madstencilist.com.

Randy Ingram and Bryan Townsend:
Randy studied at the DuCret School of Fine Art, while Brian studied at the National Academy of Design in New York City. Brain's portraits and still-life paintings are becoming prized gallery collectables. Commissions include private, corporate and museum clients. Both artists are Faux-cademy award winners. Their work has been featured in Faux Effects World, The Faux Finisher, and The Journal Magazine. The team also offers mural instruction. They donated a mural on canvas to the Chicago church project.

www.classicalartstudios.com

Artists

Patti Irwin:

Owner of Taperan Studios, Patti is a multi-talented artist, but her passion lies in creating one of a kind furniture pieces. Having trained with Pierre Finkelstein, Nicola Vigini, Jean-Pierre Besenval, and Patrick Kirwin, she is proficient in trompe l 'oeil and decorative painting. Patti painted a $10 yard sale table with vines painted to mimic the window fabric in the kitchen. The drop leaf includes a Tuscan scene. for the Arlington project. Patti also serves as Vice-Chair for the overall HTFB project bringing her superior organizational and leadership skills in to play. In addition, Patti is vice-president of her local SALI chapter, the Chesapeake Bay Stencilers.

www.taperanstudio.com

Michael Gross:

Michael's Creations founder Michael Gross began faux and decorative painting in 1994. Professionally trained by the N.Y. based "The Finishing School, Inc." and "The Academy of Wall Artistry" of Fairfax, VA, he has been an award-winning student of art from an early age, Michael has used his skills to create unique atmospheres in many forms, ranging from theatrical sets to murals and custom wall finishes. In his free time Michael enjoys figurative sculpting and woodworking. Still a student of art, he continues to enhance his abilities through continued training and frequent experimentation with new techniques and materials. He then combines these skills and artistic visions with his experience as a professional painter for truly unique and beautiful "creations". Michael completed the wine cellar cabinet, fire screen for sleeping dog, and elegant wooden trashcan for the Arlington project.

www.michaelscreations.com

Amy Ketteran:

Ketteran Studios combines Amy's classical and theatrical art training. She received her BA in Studio Art from Grinnell College, and her MFA in Scenic Art from Brandeis University. Her varied training allows her to work quickly and efficiently, without sacrificing quality and individuality. She is also a highly regarded instructor. Her teaching philosophy is based on her students learning how to see, then apply this knowledge to varied mediums. Active in the Stencilist's Artisans League, Inc. (SALI), She has served in several leadership positions and taught classes at the SALI National Convention. Amy has completely transformed the upstairs hall and stairwell of the Arlington project. She also has mentorship programs and The Business of Creativity Conferences.

www.ketteranstudios.com

www.thebizofcreativity.com

Kelly S. King:

Kelly King is one of the nation's top decorative artists/instructors. He owns the Kelly S. King Academy of Faux Painting and Decorative Finishing School, with locations in Omaha, Nebraska and Seattle, Washington. His school features classes in decorative wall finishes, furniture finishing, woodwork and cabinetry. Kelly also hosts the Faux-cademy, a national awards event for faux finishers and decorative artists. His on-line forum, www.ksknetwork.com, offers ongoing support for his students, how-tos & chats with special areas for specific products primarily: Golden, Adicolor, Perfecto & Modern Masters. Kelly's work is featured in the book's furniture chapter. Two of his signature finishes "pitted stone" and "cracked leather" were used in the wine cellar of the Arlington project.

www.in-faux.com

Melanie Kershner:

Melanie Kershner, founder of Heavenly Home Designs is a highly sought after and experienced faux finisher/muralist. She is also co-owner of Beaux-Artes. Melanie has many years experience in the art field and is well known and respected as an expert on combining different techniques and products for truly unique finishes. She often incorporates a spiritual element into her designs. Melanie created heaven in the clouds in the children's nursery, Arlington Project including the 4 walls, ceiling, and floor-cloth. Her room includes minerals added to the paints to make it glow in the dark. Her Beaux-Artes products have been featured in national publications, multiple show houses and television.

www.heavenlyhomedesigns.com

Stuart Kershner:

Stuart Kershner of Beaux-Artes, donated and applied architectural finishes to every room of the Faux House using the Beaux-Artes extensive line of architectural detailing products. HVAC vents, recessed lights covers, decorative moldings, hinge straps, and door escutcheons made a huge difference in the transformation. Stuart also used his carpentry skills for door and trim in the nursery, the overmantle and baseboards in the living room, and the wooden refrigerator panels. His efforts were critical in making the house and church transformations complete.

www.beauxartes.com

Chesna Koch:

Chesna Koch, of Chesna Koch Artistic Finishes, has been painting and creating decorative finishes since 1989. Chesna's work has become valued for its sophistication and timelessness.

She is currently enjoying a successful decorative arts service in Chicago, IL. She was in charge of the Chicago church grottesca stairwell and fellowship hallway. Her work and client homes have been featured in several showcase houses, Southern Accents, Dalas Home, Dallas Home Design, Modern Luxury Dallas, and the book Spectacular Homes of Texas.

www.chesnakoch.com

Yves Lanthier:

Born in St. Jérôme, Québec, Canada, Yves Lanthier's artwork has won multiple awards. He has been profiled in numerous publications including Florida Design, Art Business News, Palm Beach Illustrated, and Boca Raton News. Named one of the World's Best Trompe l'oeil Artists in December 2004, Yves' commissions include multi-million dollar estates such as Celine Dion's in Jupiter, Florida. He recently published The Art of Trompe L'oeil Murals. The book and large canvas reproductions of his work are available on his website. Yves' murals are featured in the Chicago church hallway (ceiling) and the church rectory's study (map).

www.yvesart.com

Ron Layman:

Ron Layman owns The Faux School with locations in Maryland and Orlando, FL offering a wide range of instruction on all elements of faux. Ron also carries products to include: Rivedil™, Adicolor, Mica Powders, MIXOL™, brushes, tools, sprayers, etc. He often brings in guest instructors such as Barth White and William Cochran . As Room Captain for the master bedroom, Ron created a truly unique and elegant room with the theme "Crossroads to Culture" which incorporated a mix of Moroccan, Moorish, Indonesian, and Indian design elements.

www.thefauxschool.com

Annie Lemarié:
Annie Lemarié is the owner of *Main Street Arts LLC*, a decorative arts studio located in central Maryland. The company offers graining, marbling, glazed and plaster wall finishes, gilding, casting, and murals. Annie often works in the exacting historic restoration arena. Her training includes a Fine Arts degree from the Maryland Institute College of Art in Baltimore, and special studies with several top artists and studios. Annie's projects have been published in The Faux Finisher, Elle Décor magazine, Frederick magazine, and Washington Home and Gardens magazine. Since 1980, she has been providing custom decorative arts for interior designers, architects and private clients in the mid-Atlantic region, and throughout the United States. Annie was the artist for the wine cellar "wooden" barrel table.

www.mainstreetarts.com

Gary Lord:
Gary Lord is recognized as an international artist, teacher, author and television personality. His work has recently been awarded seven National 1st Place awards for Best Faux Finisher of the Year. Through his school and distributorship, Prismatic Painting Studio, he can better share the real tricks of the trade and practical business knowledge he has gained in over 20 years in the field, with the students in each class. Gary is well known for selling books and DVDs that share this information. He was the Room Captain for the Chicago Project Rectory Dining Room, where he applied one of his signature metallic foil finishes.

www.prismaticstudio.com

Dan Mahlmann:
Dan Mahlmann, owner of *Decorative Concrete of Maryland, Inc.*, earned his Master's Certificate in Applications from the World of Concrete in 2005. His company specializes in decorative interior

and exterior concrete overlay applications and high-end finishes for walks, flooring, vertical walls, textures, countertops, acid stains, concrete stamping and faux rock creations. His company's work on the Arlington project includes the side landing, shed entrance, and concrete countertop in the kitchen.

www.decorativecreteofmd.com

Jne' Medellin:
Jne' Medellin began her faux career with Twin Diamonds Studio, Maryland and traveled nationwide on commissioned projects. She later started her own company in Virginia: *BG Decorative Painting Studio*. Jne's work is featured in several local restaurants, Old Town Shops, and across the United States. Jne' is trained in almost every decorative painting product line and enjoys mixing varied products for unique results. She has created several original finishes which are truly beautiful and one of a kind. Jne' is also an accomplished muralist and created the murals in the downstairs bath, which were "painted" with Behr Venetian plaster.

www.bgdecorativepaint.com

Julie Miles:
J. Miles Studios Inc., founded in 1991, is a full service decorative painting studio serving the Washington D.C. Metropolitan area and all points beyond. Dedicated to the hands-on artistry and craftsmanship of the decorative painting industry, Julie has 25 years of painting experience, a BFA from Virginia Commonwealth University, and has studied with many masters in the field. Julie is joined in the business by her husband, Brad Duerson. Brad brings his natural artistic hand as well as his diverse background in historical restoration. Together they transformed the downstairs Gentlemen's Room, Arlington project.

www.jmilesstudios.com

Michel Nadaï
A Master Artisan voted Best Craftsman of France, Michel Nadaï has over 25 years of experience in decorative painting and trompe l'oeil. He is quite well known in the both the U.S. and Europe. Besides running a successful decorative painting business, Michel has trained students from all over the world, both in his own school in the Southwest of France and in travel courses across the United States. His school offers classes in trompe-l'oeil, wood and marble graining, perspective, and painted murals.

www.michelnadai.com

Joanne Nash:
Joanne Nash is one of the top decorative artists in Virginia. She has been featured in several magazines and her award winning trompe l'oeil was featured at the International Artist Exchange in 2004. While her studio is in Gladys VA (near Lynchburg), she does a great deal of commissioned work in Smith Mt. Lake, Richmond, Washington, D.C., and California. Joanne is a favorite of top designers because she can create one of a kind signature finishes to complement any room and often brings fabric elements into hand painted wall or furniture embellishments. Having studied in Italy, she was inspired by the grotesca scroll work so popular there and incorporated it into her custom design work for the Romantic Bedroom.

www.joannenash.com

Maggie O'Neill:
With a Masters of Fine Art from the University of Georgia Cortona Italy program, Maggie was moved by the rich art history of the Renaissance. Her portfolio includes exterior murals, restaurants, shops, architectural painting, commissioned fine art, portraits, and documentary

photography. Maggie's work has been featured in several show houses and exhibits and she was selected by the D.C. Commission on the Arts and Humanities for the public art project; "Pandamania." Her services include decorative consulting, production, and decorative painting.

Maggie painted and plastered the wine cellar stairwell.www.oneillstudios.com

Leonard Pardon:
Leonard Pardon trained as an artist then was apprenticed for 7 years to British Master, A. E. Baxby. There he learned the techniques passed through the generations since the middle ages. Leonard has passed this to a new generation of students through his own teaching and his step-by-step, how-to videos. His clientele include Kings, Queens, Sultans, Sheikhs, film and rock stars. He recently had 13 of his series of videos shown nationwide by PBS. He has appeared on Discovery Channel on *Home Matters* and numerous guest appearances on overseas cable channels. Leonard used marbling and wood grain techniques on two canvas floor panels for the Chicago church.

www.pardonstudio.com

Rebecca Parsons:
Rebecca owns *Rebecca E. Parsons Studios, Inc.* in Athens, GA and Temecula, CA. Author of *"Do What You Love-Love What You Do, The Step-by-Step Guide to Faux Business,"* she conducts *Do What You Love™ Creativity Workshops*, guest instruction and motivational speaking blend deep spirituality and colorful history. She is a business consultant/coach to many artists and serves the Stencil Artisans League, Inc. (SALI) as Editor of *The Artistic Stenciler* magazine. She has appeared on HGTV and the DIY Network and writes for several publications including *The Faux Finisher* and *American Painting Contractor*.

www.fauxisme.com

Paulette Piazza:
Paulette Piazza, Denver, Colorado serves all the surrounding Rocky Mountain resorts. Her specialties are murals, frescos, trompe l'oeil, all original faux finishes, and Italian plasters.
Her extensive experience has been obtained through St. John's University, NY, the Academia Di Belle Arti in Perugia, Italy, Foreign Studies with Janet Shearer (England), and Nicola Vigini, (Italy), as well as an apprenticeship with William Cochran and intensive workshops at the nation's top faux schools. Paulette transformed the Chicago study/ library child's room in Church of the Atonement in Chicago.

www.piazzartist.com

Jacek Prowinski:
As an experienced artisan, Jacek Prowinski focuses on the details while preserving the authenticity of historic structures and churches. He has a teaching degree and is a graduate of a professional painting school. He teaches faux painting workshops ranging from one-day to five-day comprehensive training sessions. Co-owner of *Faux Design Studio* in Addison, Illinois, Jacek has directed crews on-site for both residential and commercial commissions. Jacek has been profiled in a number of publications including *The Faux Finisher, Profiles In Faux Finishing* and *Faux Effects World*. He has been featured on episodes of HGTV's *New Spaces* program and is well known throughout Chicago and US for his church commissions. Jacek was selected to work his magic on the Chicago Church Narthex, which adjoins the Sanctuary.

www.fauxdesignstudio.com

Donna Phelps
Donna Phelps is owner and principle instructor of The Sarasota School of Decorative Arts, Inc. Her style is fresh and cutting edge. She has more than 18 years of training and experience in

both old world techniques and new age products which ensures her students receive a wealth of real world knowledge, technical support, and the unique opportunity to learn to execute complex finishes. Donna is a very popular instructor at the Stencil Artisan's League International conferences, the annual "Faux Event ", and is often asked to teach at other schools across the country and internationally. She is also much sought after by designers for her one of a kind finishes and her new stencil line. She completed the beautiful palm frond finish in the Master bath.

www.ssda1.com

Melanie Royals:
Melanie Royals is the President/Creative Director of *Royal Design Studio*, an industry leader known for creating innovative and elegant stencil designs and techniques. Her work, art, and "Extraordinary Stenciled Effects" program have helped to raise stenciling to the higher level of appreciation and application that it has become today. Most recently she has taken decorative pattern application to an even broader level by introducing Modello Designs® - decorative masking pattern, custom-sized adhesive designs that have revolutionized the industry. Melanie shares her passion and knowledge through an acclaimed video series, books, workshops, television appearances and regular magazine articles. She transformed the living room floor and donated several Modellos® to the Faux House.

www.royaldesignstudio.com

Kathleen A. Sakry
It all started when Kathleen became an apprentice to a fellow decorative artist. As she gained in skill, it was apparent that this was the career she wanted. Having studied under one of the leading decorative art institutes, she continues her education to further develop the hand. As proficiency continues to increase, she writes columns in a leading architecture and design trade magazine, appears as a quest on home decorating programs and on radio programs. Kathleen took a national award for her work. The new challenges that appear almost daily add fuel to her enthusiasm.

kathleensakry @ frontiernet.net

Andreas Scholz
Born and raised in Calgary, Andreas began painting at an early age and continued through graduation from the Southern Alberta Institute of Technology. His specialized art training includes some of the best US schools: SAIT, Vandalae Studios in Seattle, Vigini Studios in San Antonio, and The Finishing School in New York and Pennsylvania. His business: *Artistic Finishes by Andreas*, specializes in European finishes and art. His work has been showcased in the Parade of Homes winning Trillium, Reggie Design, and People's Choice awards around the Twin Cities. Andreas donated a mural for the auction which is featured in the murals and floor cloth chapter.

www.finishesbyandreas.com

Tania Seabock:
Tania Seabock of *Seabock Studios* is one of the most acclaimed decorative/restorative artists in the Washington D.C. metro area. She works in many mediums including gilding, sculpting, glass, mold 0making/casting, plasters, and painting. She graduated from The Nadaï-Verdon Advanced School of Decorative Painting in the southwest of France and specializes in wood grain, marble, gilding, compo, and ceiling design. Tania works with her husband Ian, who specializes in mold making and casting, glass, bronze, plasters. She served as Room Captain for the dining room and Room Lt. for the Gentlemen's Room. She is also part of the DPAP apprenticeship program and has several how-to DVDs available through www.fauxhouse.com.

www.seabockstudios.com

Ashley Spencer
C. Ashley Spencer grew up in the flamboyant and artistic city of New Orleans. She still has a strong connection to her hometown and is excited to help them rebuild by participation in this project.

A graduate, with a degree in Art History and a minor in Fine Arts, from The University of the South, Ashley also studied at Parsons in Paris and the Washington, D.C Concoran Gallery of Art. She has worked at the National Gallery of Art, Design and Installation Department, National Gallery Of Women in the Arts-Exhibition Design Department, and at Washington, D.C.'s Arena Stage as a scenic painter. She was the graphic artist/ illustrator for Consumers' Research Magazine for 15 years. Ashley attributes her success to her talented art teachers, her study and appreciation of art history, and her strong background in drawing, from which every good painting derives.

www.ashley-spencer.com.

Francesca Springolo:
Born in Milan, Italy, Francesca Springolo had a great passion for painting from an early age. She graduated from the "Scuola del Fumetto" in Milan and became an illustrator. The opportunity to work on a large-scale project materialized in the spring of 1996 and since then she has traveled the world decorating restaurants, hotels and private homes in Italy, Germany, Mexico and the United States. She met her husband Geoff in Venice, Italy in the summer of 2000 and then moved to the United States, settling in Bethesda MD. Francesca completed a trompe l'oeil panel for the romantic bedroom fireplace and the donkey for the shed/home studio in Arlington.

www.francescaspringolo.com

Mary Steingesser:
Mary Steingesser of *ArtZMary Studio* is the Room Captain in charge of the Arlington home office/artist studio. This room, once a shed, was a huge challenge. Mary brought together a diverse group of artists from SALI and other artist friends to complete a whimsical room decorated with several complicated murals. She even created the ceiling moldings and hand painted the framed flower paintings. Mary has a BA from the University of New Hampshire and is an accomplished artist specializing in fine art-but her passion is abstract art and sculpture. Her works have been displayed in many shows and galleries in the DC area.

www.artzmary.com

Wanda Timmons:
Wanda Timmons, has over 18 years experience in wall finishes and owns *Designer Finishes, Inc.*, an Aqua Finishing Solutions™ Studio in Warrensburg, IL. She has pioneered incredibly realistic and beautiful finishes for countertops, furniture, and floors. Wanda's work has been featured in model homes in Chatham and Champaign, IL and in the 2004 Showcase of Homes in Mahomet, IL. Her school of faux finishes is well known for exciting and unique finishes. Her Venetian plaster kitchen countertop in the Arlington Project looks just like granite and the marmarino countertop in the wine cellar fooled even a tile contractor!

www.wandafaux.com

Justin Valez-Hagen:
Justin Valez-Hagen, owner of *DC Concrete Technologies* has over 10 years of experience in the construction industry. A self-proclaimed "creative entrepreneur," Justin has started several companies and enjoys the opportunity his new company affords him to custom design concrete projects. He is also working towards earning an MBA and Law Degree from George Washington University and has plans to expand the company to several other cities. He and his crew completely transformed the front walk and entrance of the house and kitchen floor.

www.dcconcretetechnologies.com

Adrienne van Dooren
Adrienne van Dooren, Project Chair and author of *The House That Faux Built* is an experienced faux finisher, artist, instructor and speaker. She has trained under master artisans in both the US and Europe and her work has been featured in numerous magazines and TV. She accepts only 1-2 commissions a year, preferring to coach beginning artists, teach, speak and participate in charity projects.

www.cefaux.com
www.fauxhouse.com

Carol van Gerena:
Carol van Gerena of *Red Lion Stencils* completed a canvas panel for the Chicago Church Project using the Red Lion line of Stencils. The panel is 3 x 4' of a crane in water and surrounded with Beaux-Artes molding. Carol's stencil line has many elements perfect for murals such as fountains, archways etc, great designs for children's rooms and much more. She also has smaller stencils created just for scrap booking and smaller projects. Using these stencils with a bit of hand embellishing and shading results in a work of art.

www.redlionstencils.com

Nicola Vigini
A native Italian, Nicola attended the prestigious Liceo Artistico in Rome and the Institute Superieure de Peintre Decorative in Paris, He combines a lifetime of artistic training in Europe and America, and is best known as a master of trompe l'oeil and grotesca. His wife Leslie is his business partner and innovative instructor of fine finishes at their studio in San Antonio, TX. Together they host an annual painting trip to Italy with top guest instructors for an unforgettable experience. Nicola recently released a new line of grotesca stencils and furnished stunning grotesca panels to the Arlington and Chicago projects.

www.viginistudios.com

Barth White:
With over 20 years experience in faux finishing, Barth White is best known for his incredible work in casinos in Las Vegas, the faux capitol of the world. Barth invented the Faux Tool and teaches faux finishing and decorative painting at *Barth's Faux Studio* in Las Vegas and all across the country. His clients include such world renowned casinos as Caesar's Palace, Rio, Bellagio, Venetian, Paris, Aladdin, and the new Wynn hotel in Las Vegas. Barth applied marmarino to the walls and a glazed faux finish to the ceiling of the Arlington living room. He also fauxed and distressed the dated fireplace, molding and doors.

www.faux.com

Rose Wilde
Rose and Jack Wilde founded the Wood Icing Company in 2000. It became Rose's brainchild when she discovered this new way to add dimension and texture to furniture. She quickly discovered that others found her invention to be so intriguing, that she now has a patent pending. The day she invented the Wood Icing technique, she knew she was onto something big. It was unique, versatile, and durable. She made piece after piece, impressing her friends and family and newfound clients. The word spread quickly, and soon she received client referrals and calls from decorators asking for custom pieces. This newfound passion of hers was a hit. Now, she and her husband, Jack, manage The Wood Icing Company full time and teach technique classes across the country. Rose remade the ugly metal cabinet in the shed. She has a how-to video on wood-icing technique available through www.fauxhouse.com.

www.woodicing.com

Caroline Woldenberg:
Caroline Woldenberg began her career as a interior designer, then found her passion for painting in 1987. Her projects have taken her throughout the United States, as well as to the Marias district of Paris and the fashion district of Milan. Based in Atlanta, her company has been servicing the area's top designers as a full service decorative arts company for residential, large commercial and religious installations. Their services include wall finishes, plastering, murals, painted furnishings, and gilding. Caroline has a reputation as one of the best faux and furniture instructors in the country. Her work has been featured in Southern Accents, Veranda, and House Beautiful. She is the designer and finisher for the Arlington kitchen.

www.thefinishingschoolatl.com

Josh Yavelberg:
At the age of thirteen, Josh Yavelberg began studying the human figure at the University of Miami under the instruction of professor Luis Ulman. He later studied at Pratt Institute for Art and Design in Brooklyn, New York where he obtained a B.S. as well as a Master's Degree in Art History. Josh currently lives in the Washington, D.C. Metro area pursuing his own artwork as well as portrait and mural commissions. While incorporating his knowledge of art history with his artwork, much of his work has been described as "ambitious" and "impressive." The main goal has been to provide the viewer with an opportunity to interact and connect with his works of art while expressing the world from a unique point of view. Josh painted the woman in towel, basement closet, Arlington.

www.yavelbergstudios.com

Small Spaces:

Shawn Bessenyei
half bath
703 209-7722

Carol Patterson
right hall closet
www.carolswallsoffaux.com

Lisa Turner
left hall closet
elegantfauxdesign@yahoo.com

Tracie Weir
basement bath
www.novafauxcreations.com

Designers:

Mau-Don Nuyen
Growing up in Viet-Nam during the war, Mau-Don's house was totally destroyed by bombs. "The house that Mau-Don and family rebuilt" was started from scratch. She "painted" every corner of the house with color chalks, egg white, and clay. That was the dawn of Mau-Don's passion for decorative painting. After being a software engineer for 25 years, Mau-Don decided to study interior design, and is now realizing her childhood dream in painting. Her company, *Painted Sky Interiors*, creates harmonies of different cultures in clients' homes, using paint and art work from the near West and the far East. Mau-Don and Nancy AtLee selected the perfect furniture and accessories to complement the faux for *The House That Faux Built.*

wwwpaintedskyinteriors.com

Nancy AtLee
Nancy AtLee Interiors opened its doors concentrating on freelance interior design services. Since then Nancy has been involved with many interior design projects, residential and commercial. She was recently awarded the "Peoples Choice Award" for her work in a Charity Home Tour, a national award for a design project using Jan Dressler Stencils, and she has been featured in several national magazines. While business was her major in college, she minored in interior design. Her love of faux finishes developed 5 years ago. "I wanted to show my clients how they could enhance their walls, floors, etc with faux finishes instead of just paint." Nancy was asked to participate as an interior designer on the Faux House because of her magical pairing of faux finishes and interior design.

www.nancyatleeinteriors.com

Photographers

Dave Galen
Dave Galen, Leesburg VA, specializes in advertising, architecture, interiors, corporate, and industrial photography. His photographs have won awards repeatedly for his clients from the Associated Builders and Contractors, The National Commercial Builders Council, and The Northern Virginia Building Industry Association. His photos have been featured in 3 books: *The House that Faux Built, Loudoun County—Blending Tradition with Innovation,* and *Loudoun—A Photographic Portrait,* which highlights Loudoun County's 250th anniversary. Dave is also a contributing editorial photographer in: *The Loudoun County Volunteer Rescue Squad* and several national magazines. Dave is currently working on a national campaign promoting public awareness with the Brain Injury Association of America.

www.galenphoto.com.

Omar Salinas:
Born in Bolivia, Omar Salinas, owner of Hi Tech Photo grew up in New York City. As a portrait photographer at Harris and Ewing, he photographed the Nation Capital's powerful & elite in government and business. Eventually he found his niche in architectural photography. In his 30 years of experience, he has brought his talent and exquisite taste for design contrast, tones, and richness of colors to each of his works of art. He has mastered lighting and all camera formats, including digital imaging. Omar's work has been published in several magazines showcasing most of D.C.'s finest homes.
www.hitechphotousa.com

Contributors:
In progress photography by: Suzanne Leedy, Ceil Glembocki, Lisa Turner, Tracie Wier, Tania Seabock, Ashley Spencer, and Louise Kraft.

Volunteers:

100-Hour Volunteer Artists:

Carl Bayer
www.fauxandfleur.com

Ceil Glembloci
virginiaeggcouncil@erols.com

Andra Held
andraot@comcast.com

Lorre lei Jackson
editing

Patti Newton
www.elephantsonthe wall.com

Linda ONeill
www.artbyoneill.com

Caroline Spencer
carolynspencer12@yahoo.com

Celeste Stewart
cstewart999@gmail.com

Lisa Turner
elegantfauxdesign@yahoo.com

Tracie Weir
www.Novafauxcreations.com

Other Volunteers

Sandi Anderson	Hope Gibbs	Stacey Matarese	Piers Spencer
Sheri Anderson	Simona Grigorjevaite	Rosalie Myers	Karen Steele
Christine Barnette	Susan Guarino	Kate Nagle	Marc Steingesser
Mike Bedster	Joan Hagan	Laura Nalley	Rachel Steingesser
Khacki Berry	Lee Hickman	Dennis Nash	Vicki Suazo
Carolyn Blahosky	Susan Huber	Patrick O'Neill	Amanda Summerlin
Steve Brown	Ryoko Kanker	David Reyes	Wanda Swierczynski
Michele Cady	Emily Kato	Cathi Rinn	Debbie Thompson
Heavenly Campbell	Kathy Keel	Carol Rohrbaugh	Barb Tise
Kathy Carroll	Mark Ketteran	Ian Seabock	Robert Turner
Melissa Clements	Li Lammert	Russell Sellineer	Jenny Vanier-Walter
Ann Cook	Elizabeth Lee	Jacky Shaw	Sharon VanMeter
Sandra Davis	John Leonard	Sue Sidun	Joanne Voll
Jenna DeFalco,	Lewis Lewis	Pauline Siple	Eric Whiteside
Debbie Dennis	Hector Lopez	Jennifer Skene	Chris Woodruff
Ernie Dominguez	Jonathon Lutz	Sally Skene	Belinda Yoder
Mitch Eanes	Denise Malueg	Donna Smith	
Carol Farley	Linda Manning	Francesca Springolo	
Reginal Flemming	Sylvia Martorana	Peter Spencer	

Landscaper:

Chris Jackson
Landscaper Chris Jackson of R.C. Jackson Landscaping Inc. used his decades of experience (and a bit of magic!) to transform patches of dirt and weeds into a haven of flowers, scrubs, iron and stone. Like a conductor with his symphony, he brought harmony to the house and grounds. Chris donates many hours to Artists4Others building water features for hospice. He is passionate about cob homes and other "green" building methods.

www.RCJacksonlandscaping.com

A sincere thank you to all our sponsors. Without you there would be no "House that Faux Built" and a special thanks to our platinum sponsors bolded below for your generous support.

PLATINUM SPONSORS:

Andreae Designs
Artimatrix
Ashley Spencer
Barth White/Barth's Faux Studio
Beaux-Artes Faux and Moldings
BG Decorative Paint
Creative Enterprises
Crosby Amblard Studios
Designer Finishes
Elephants on the Wall
Fauxcademy
Faux and Fleur
Faux Design Studio
Faux Effects®, International
The Faux School
The Finishing Source, Atlanta
Heavenly Home Designs
High-Tec Photography
Jmiles Studios
Kelly S. King Institute of Fine Finishes
Ketteran Studios
The Mad Stencilist
TheMuralSchool
Mary Stengesser
Modello® Designs
O'Neill Studios
Nancy and Walt Petrie
Paintin the Town Faux
Prismatic Painting Studios
RMR Associates
Royal Design Studio
Sarasota School of Decorative Arts, Inc.
Seabock Studios
Suzanne Leedy-McEnearney Associates
Taperan Studio
Thompson Creek Windows
Vigini Studios

GOLD
Exquisite Finishes
Chris Jackson Landscaping
Keep My Pet
Kingslan & Gibilisco Decorative Arts
Pierre Finkelstein Inst. of Dec. Painting
Leonard Pardon
Roc-Lon
The Wood Icing Company

SILVER:
Callico Corners
Classical Art Studios
Michel Nadai
Oriental Rugs and More
Patricia's Palette
Red Lion Stencils
Stencil Planet

BRONZE:
Adicolor
Anything But Plain
Arlington Paint & Decorating Center
Art Stuf
Behr Paints
Buon Fresco
Color Wheel Paints and Coatings:
 • Adicolor
 • Benjamin Moore
 • Briste Group
 • Modern Masters
 • Oikos
 • Skimstone
Coral Light
Creative Evolutions
DC Concrete Technologies
Decorative Concrete of Maryland, Inc
Dominion Floors
Faux by Kathy
Faux like a Pro

Golden Artist Colors, Inc.
Joe Grecco
Hanging Treasures
Krylon Paints
Liliandahl Studios
Noland Plumbing Supplies
Oriental Rugs and More
Patina Studios
Priscilla Houser
Media Connections
PROFAUX
Red Hot Copy
School of Italian Plasters
Sphinx Oriental Weavers
Star Catering
Stencilworks
Steven List
Vendelay Marketing Firm
Wing Enterprises
York Graphic Services
Yves Art

GENERAL:
Action Iron, LLC
AMPS Industries, Inc.
Art by O'Neill
Bella Vernici Studios
Benjamin Moore Paints
Bray and Scarff, Lee Hwy
Brown Construction
Buckingham Stencils
Calvert's Fountains and Ponds
Ceil Glembocki
Curtain, Furniture & Upholstery, LLC
Color Alchemist School & Restoration
Daige Pro-cote Waxer
Decofinish
Discount Fabrics USA
Donna's Designs
Exquisite-Finishes
Faux Fingers
Faux Mart
Faux Products
Gallen Photography
Hanging Treasures
Hatchers Floors
Heart of the Home Stencils
Jan Dresler Stencils

Julie Kriss, McEnearney Associates, Inc
Kenny Hopel
Kim Wadford
Karibeth Creations
Jon P. Lutz
Rebecca Hotop
Sherwin-Williams Company, Fairfax, VA
Parvati Textures.com
Priscilla Hauser
Hope Gibbs
Jan Dressler Designs
Jennifer-Rebecca Designs
Tim and Marie Tibor
MZ Drapery Accents
Laser Excel
Liliedahl Fine Art Studio
Luminex USA
Lynn Brehm Stencils
Murals Your Way
McEnearney Associates
Patina studios ltd
Pure Texture
Plaza Arts
Roma International
Scentco
Schmitt, Dorothy, Landscape Design
Sherwin Williams International
Sinopia
The Stenciled Garden
Stencil Kingdom
Susie-Darrell-Smith
Ed Swartout
Terra Bella Finishes
Tim Poe-Antique Mirror Patina Solution
Tust Studio
Twig and a Feather, Inc.
Vintage Homes of Wichita
Wall Transformation Designs
Westover Florist
Wing Enterprises
ZB Kids Designs

Work in Progress

126

Painting 101 - The basics make all the difference

This is the most important, yet ignored process. The most beautiful faux and plasters can peel right off if the base coating is poorly done ,you use the wrong type of tape, or don't use the correct type of primer.

6 STEPS TO PROPER PREPARATION AND BASE COATING:

1. EXAMINE YOUR WALLS.

Spackle holes, sand previous drips, etc, to make the wall is smooth to paint. Always spot prime over spackle.

2. SELECT A COLOR.

This sounds easy but often isn't. There are dozens of variations of white alone.

- *Select on a general color*–Go for sample swatches or packets.
- *Decide between cool or warm*–Cool colors tend to have more blue in them (e.g. greens, some browns, etc.) and generally recede which can make a room appear larger. Warm colors have more red and/or yellow. They tend to feel more cozy. However, there is also a range of warmth within a selection of cool or warm colors. For example, a red that is close to orange is a warm red, while a burgundy is a cooler red.
- *If matching a fabric, take it with you.* Don't depend on memory. You'll need to hold it against the swatches or have it color-matched by computer.
- *Remember that colors often look darker when applied to an entire wall.* On the other hand, a dark chip held against a white wall will appear far darker than it really is. Be brave.

3. SELECT THE PROPER SHEEN.

- *Ceiling paint*–ultra-flat paint used to hide ceiling imperfections
- *Flat*–reflects the least light. This is a big advantage if your walls are less than perfect. Flat is considered the most "upscale" for living rooms, dining rooms, bedrooms, etc. The disadvantage of flat paint is that it is very porous and therefore difficult to clean, and is generally a poor surface for faux glaze finishes.
- *Satin and Eggshell*–There is a slight difference in the two, but not much. Satin and eggshell paints reflect a bit more light, and are easier to clean. Since they are less porous, they provide a good surface for most faux finishes. The disadvantage is that wall imperfections such as patches and drips show up more.
- *Semi-gloss*–Most popular finish for trim and sometimes used in bathrooms, kitchens, and small children's rooms. Semi-gloss reflects light and is very washable. The disadvantage is that it highlights imperfections and looks institutional on entire walls.
- *Gloss*–normally reserved for trim, has a high gloss and is washable.
- *Textured*–includes sand or other additives to create texture.

4. BUY THE BEST QUALITY PAINT, PRIMER AND BRUSHES YOU CAN AFFORD.

In the long run it will save you time and money. Less costly paints have fewer solids, and therefore don't cover as well, often requiring an extra coat of paint for the same coverage as higher quality paint. Also, thinner paint is more likely to drip. The same rule generally applies to brushes, particularly angle brushes. Cheap brushes tend to shed more and not last as long. Inexpensive roller covers sometimes have visible seams that form a pattern on the wall.

5. DETERMINE WHETHER A PRIMER IS NEEDED AND, IF SO, WHAT TYPE.

Not all primers are the same; there are different types for different purposes.

Always prime when:

- *The previous paint was an oil paint, and you plan to use a water-based product.* Most acrylic/latex paints do not adhere well to oil-based paints. (They may appear to at first, but will peel later.) To determine whether a wall was last painted in oils, rub a bit of denatured alcohol over one spot. If the paint comes off, it is water-based; if it does not come off, it is likely oil, but to be sure you may try a bit of paint thinner–it will remove oil paint. Ironically there are water-based and oil-based primers that will bond well with an acrylic top-coat (read the label to be sure.)
- *The surface is stained with water, smoke etc.* (use a sealing primer).
- *Painting over fresh drywall* (use only primer made for this purpose).
- *Spackling (you must at least spot prime over the spackle).*
- *Painting over a previously sealed, varnished or shiny surface* BIN primer works well even over plastic and silicone. There are several primers specifically made for plastic, glass, metal, rust and/or tile. It is usually best to lightly sand or etch these very slick surfaces or use a chemical etcher for max adhesion.
- *Painting raw or knotted wood* Raw wood requires sandable primer because the primer's moisture will raise the grain and should then be sanded smooth. If the wood has knots, use a specialty sealing primer to prevent them from bleeding through the paint.
- *Painting over a previous texture* or plaster such as Lusterstone®
- *Improving the bonding qualities of the wall*–If in doubt, prime!
- *Painting over wallpaper.* It is usually best to remove the paper, but should you choose to paint, first glue down any loose seams, then use a paintable calk or spackle to hide the seam lines and top with an oil based primer so that you don't loosen the glue.

Note: It is also a good idea to prime when using a light color paint over a very dark coat and keep in mind primer can be tinted closer to the new wall color. Remember there are many types of primer–be sure to discuss your needs with a paint professional to ensure you buy the correct type.

6. PREPARE THE ROOM:

- *Remove furniture* or move larger pieces to the center of the room and cover
- *Tape down heavy paper to protect the floors.* Special coated paper in large rolls is available at paint stores. Paper has many advantages over plastic or drop cloths. First, it is less likely to cause you or the ladder to slip. Second, if taped properly, it is less likely to pull away from the wall and it is easier to detect spills. The cleanup is easy, no tarps with wet paint going in your car–just roll the paper up and throw it away.
- *Clean the surface.* This step is often ignored but is very important. Take a bucket of water and add TSP (available at paint and hardware stores). TSP removes any oils or residues left behind by kitchen grease, cleaners or fingers. Oils, dust, and spiderwebs are often present on the walls, and particularly the baseboards, making it difficult for the tape and paint to adhere properly.
- *Tape* off the area you do not want painted such as baseboards, the ceiling line, etc. Use a very, very low tack painters tape. Never use masking tape. Most people assume all blue 3M tape is low-tack, however there are two types. The cheaper tape has a rough feel to it and is sold for and often used for painting. However, this tape will often pull paint off as you remove it. The rough tape also bleeds under more readily than the smooth blue tape. Use it only on taping the floor, etc where there is no danger of pulling off paint. The smooth blue tape, often called 3M "orange core" tape because the center cardboard is orange, is the best tape for faux finishing. There are other brands that make a white version; just make sure it is extra low-tack. The brown paper tape is very low-tack as well, and gives a nice sharp edge. It is often used for

ceiling and stripes, but it is so low-tack that it often falls down unless reinforced with other tape.

- **Be sure to tape straight along the edge.** Crooked tape make crooked paint lines–be precise. Expert tapers try to use one continuous piece of tape, rather than tearing it so they don't have overlap lines. An added benefit is that the tape pulls down easier at the end. (There are tape holders that make that easier.)
- **Use plastic sheeting to cover walls,** if there is concern about protecting against drips or spray. It is available in rolls with tape already attached at one end.
- **Burnish the tape down** with a fingernail, credit card or plastic putty knife. For added protection, paint a thin line of clear sealer or glaze around the edge.

7. PREPARE THE PAINT.

If you buy paint at the paint store, ensure they put it in the shaking chamber. Older paint you have at home is fine, but it has likely separated to some degree; mix it with a paint stick or large spoon, or better yet a drill mixer. Inexpensive plastic attachments that fit any drill are cheap and easily available. You can also add scents or additives at this stage. (See tips.)

8. PAINT

- **Cut in with a brush.** Using an angled paint brush, paint the areas that are too close to the tape line to get with a roller. Do no more than a wall at a time because it is important to blend with the roller while the paint is still wet. A helpful tool is a masking shield, a long straight metal tool that keeps you from hitting the ceiling with your brush.
- **Roll.** Select the proper roller cover for your walls (smooth, rough, etc). Use a paint tray and don't overload the roller or you may get splatters and drips. Add a splatter guard and extension pole if painting the ceiling and wear a hat.
- **Apply a second coat if necessary.** If changing the wall color, a second coat is often required. For faux basecoats, 2 coats are recommended so you don't have missed spots that absorb the glass differently, ruining your finish.
- **Cleanup.** Have large contractor trash bags available. Cut tape if required. Pull the tape very slowly pulling it down at a 5 or 7 o'clock angle. Should it start to peel off the paint, stop and use a razor blade to recut the tape at that point. (See tips for easy clean-up ideas.)

Tips from the Pros

Place non slip-rug mats under your ladder to keep it from moving. (Tracey Weir)

Wet brushes before you use them and paint will be less likely to be sucked up into the ferrel.

Paint barefoot–when there aren't any sharp objects around, painting barefoot is a good way to feel if you have dripped any paint. You can easily wipe it off and eliminate the risk of tracking paint through the house. If you do drip on the floorcloth clean it up or cover with towels to avoid stepping in it. (Tiffany Hakimipour)

To keep roller covers soft, soak in water mixed with a little Downey and they will clean up more easily. Once clean, place one end in a glass of water and let sit for approximately 30 min. This allows any remaining paint to leach out. To keep badger and other expensive brushes soft, use creme rinse. (Adrienne van Dooren)

Never spray paint with the air ventilation system on–you can get paint in every room in the house! (Adrienne van Dooren)

Preventing rust and particles from getting into paint and glazes: For paint cans that are relatively full but are already rusting on inside, line top area of can opening with a quadruple folded plastic wrap square. Place over opening, close lid on top of this, and seal edges of wrap around can with painters tape. This will prevent rust particles from falling in can each time it's opened and before paint can be strained into a clean container. (Ashley Spencer)

Spray Pam inside your trash bags and your tapes won't stick–they fall to the bottom of the bag. (Kathy Carroll)

If you've allowed paint to dry on a brush or tools, don't despair, they may still be salvageable. Soak them in of undiluted Crud Cutter or Simple Green overnight (or longer if need be) then wash . (Joanne Nash)

Catch the Drips - Take a piece of brown paper tape and fold it in half lengthwise. Position it immediately under the section you are painting, allowing it to catch any drips. (Tiffany Hakimipour)

Lining your paint tray with Press and Seal makes clean up real easy. Sealing your product with Press and Seal before putting the lid back on and it will last a very long time. (Kathy Carroll)

Safety: Be very careful with petroleum based products (such as tinted waxes) rags left overnight can self combust; place in water until you can properly dispose of them. Do not wash paint thinners, oxidizers or plasters down the sink; you can damage pipes.

Clean oil brushes with mineral oil or even cooking oil to avoid heavy chemicals.

Keep brushes and rollers from drying out–when you take a break or finish for the day, place your paintbrush (or rollers) in a plastic bag (or use plastic wrap or press and seal) to keep out air. For even more protection, store them in a refrigerator. This will keep the brushes fresh and eliminate the need to clean them at the end of each day. This tip works for your larger brushes. Any expensive smaller brushes should be cleaned as usual. (Tiffany Hakimipour)

Tips From The Pros

Synthetic plasters adhere to flat base coats better. (Tracey Weir)

Avoid white pallet paper–it fools your eye into thinking all your colors are too dark. Instead, use a mid-toned grey or wood pallet. If you can't find grey, place grey paper under a piece of glass. (Robert Warren)

TAPE:
If blue tape looses its stickiness, simply microwave the roll for 3 seconds. If you are having difficulty removing tape, use a hair dryer to heat up the glue and make removal easier. Store leftover tape in a zip-lock bag to keep the edges from drying out. (Lisa Turner)

Put your acrylic plasters into a zip lock bag, cut one corner and squeeze out onto your trowel... great for classroom environment. (Kathy Carroll)

Spray Pam inside your trash bags and your tapes won't stick; they fall to the bottom of the bag. Kathy Carroll

Record all paint mixes and their proportions as you're working for reference. (Ashley Spencer)

Storing   & Mixing Paints:
Easy way to mix decorative finishing paints and glazes, stLine a clean, leftover, aluminum food container with heavy duty aluminum foil. This is a larger surface area than a palette but not as large as a paint tray and not heavy or cumbersome to hold and carry up a ladder. Mix paints and glazes in this with a paint stick and tear another sheet of aluminum foil to cover and press over container to seal and prevent paints from drying out while breaking. Can french-fold packet to seal overnight and use to remember paint color mixes for extended use and reference. (Ashley Spencer)

Polishing.
When polishing Venetiano or other lime based polished plasters, sand quickly with 600 grit sandpaper, followed by 2000 grit available at auto paint supply stores. Use a palm sander or even a car polisher for a high shine.

Learn about VOCC ratings and green painting products. Many paint fumes can be very hazardous to your health with repeated exposure. (Adrienne van Dooren)

Allow enough dry time for glazes. They take approximately 24 hours to fully dry and can take longer in humid weather. (Lisa Turner)

Cleaning up after plasters: When using plasters or any product you don't want to wash down a drain .... simply put a 5 gallon heavy duty trash bag into a 5 gal bucket. Add water to 1/3-1/2 of bucket and do all your washing of trowels into this. Let it sit for several days to let all the "material" settle to the bottom of the bucket. At that time, pull out the bag, poke a hole a couple of inches above the "settled material" and drain the bag. Then just toss the bag of material into the trash or dispose of according to IAW legal requirements. (Nancy Schnell)

Run a thin line of clear top coat along your ceiling line and tape line you won't seep. You must cut with a razor or sharp knife before removing tape. When removing tape after a plaster finish, run the edge of a putty knife into the seam of the tape edge to break the bond between the plaster material and the tape so it will be easier to remove. (Kathy Carroll)

Should you spill water-based paint on carpet, flood with water and keep blotting it up; I once got an entire bucket of paint out by doing this and then steam-cleaning it. However, if it is only a tiny drop or two, you can let it dry and cut it out with scissors (Kim Wadford)

Adding denatured alcohol to a glazed finish will give the finish a more aged looked. Flick with fingers lightly. (Tracey Weir)

Go online to all the faux and art forums—learn tips and ask advise!

When using a badger on wet acrylic glazes, keep a rag with denatured alcohol handy to wipe the brush and keep it clean; also keep a hair dryer handy in case it gets too damp. (Kelly King)

Be sure to check the cure time of paints and glazes—most take days or weeks to cure and will be vulnerable in the meantime.

To avoid lines in your work: You must maintain a "wet edge" to prevent any cold joints (hard lines) from forming as you work from one area to another. Make sure you work in an "organic" pattern to minimize hard wall lines and blend the edges out to almost nothing then bring the next section back into it. (Lisa Turner)

To keep roller covers soft, soak in water mixed with a little Downey and they will clean up more easily. Once clean, place one end in a glass of water and let sit for 30 minutes or longer. This allows any remaining paint to leach out. To keep badger and other expensive brushes soft, use creme rinse. (Adrienne van Dooren)

Storing & Mixing Paints:
Easy way to mix decorative finishing paints and glazes: first line a clean, leftover, aluminum food container with heavy-duty aluminum foil. This is a larger surface area than a palette but not as large as a paint tray and not heavy or cumbersome to hold and carry up a ladder. Mix paints and glazes in this with a paint stick, and tear another sheet of aluminum foil to cover and press over container to seal and prevent paints from drying out during break-times. Can french-fold packet to seal overnight, and use to remember paint color mixes for extended use and reference. (Ashley Spencer)

For artists brushes for oils, keep their shape and keep them from drying out by applying petro-leum jelly (Jennifer Carrasco)

Don't view others' faux finishers as competition. There is enough work for everyone. Share recipes, products and ideas. Work together on projects, Refer work to one another. Those who don't share, shrivel, those who share, expand.

20 paint additives to try:

anti-mildew
scent
texture
pearlescent
magnetic
lime additives
glaze
water
extender
mica powders
universal tints
dryers
flatening agent
activators
denatured alcohol
blending solvents
flow agents
glow minerals

To easily remove wall-paper, combine Joy dish detergent and water in a spray bottle and spray on wallpaper. Removal will be much easier. (Tracey Weir)

Use water with caulk for a smoother look. (Tracey Weir)

New specialty paints:

stripable fx texture
green and VOCC lines
black light paint
glow in dark minerals
chalkboard paint
"liquid" stainless steel
metallics that rust or age with acid/activators
iridescence
specialty paints for plastic, glass, metal and non-fired ceramics
heat set oil

Submit your tips for the next edition! www.fauxhouse.com

Record all paint mixes and their proportions as you're working for reference. (Ashley Spencer)

GLAZES:
Glazes extend the working time of paint. Some have more "open" or working time than others. Some product lines have extend-ers to add more time. In very warm dry weather, the glaze may dry too quickly. A humidifier and AC in the room can help. Another trick to extend glaze is to "slip coat" the wall with clear glaze before adding your paint and glaze mixture. (This also works over flat paint—but add a bit of water.) A cool room works best. (Lisa Turner)

15 WAYS TO MAKE A SMALL ROOM APPEAR LARGER:

1. Mirrors can visually double a space. Use mirrors in new ways, A faux arched doorway with a mirror can look as if there is a room beyond, mirrored tables and chests are increasingly popular, use mirrors squares or mosaics in headboards or backsplashes, the rear walls of book shelves, etc. Try mosaic and broken mirrors (remember the mailbox in the shed chapter?)
2. If you don't want mirrors use clear or colored glass, metallics etc that reflect and bounce light.
3. Clear Plexiglas or glass furniture (e.g. a glass topped dining room table) allows you to see the room or floor beyond visually increasing space
4. Monochromatic color schemes help the eye flow through the space.
5. Built-ins such as the bench seat in the kitchen, bookshelves, and murphy beds help expand space. Built-ins hide behind roll away book shelves, or can be made into a side console.
6. Check out mini-appliances
7. Look at multi-task pieces: an ottoman with storage, soda bed, washing machine that also drys, a microwave convection oven, etc. Go to an RV or boat show-many of their space-making tricks can also work at home.
8. Avoid large patterns. Use more texture for interest instead.
9. Open up the curtains, or if it's in your budget, replace a window with french doors or a bay window. Not only does the light help, but when you can see outside the space can visually double.
10. Don't have a window? Make one with a mural or mirrors behind a window frame.
11. Take the doors off of book shelves or kitchen cabinets and leave open or add glass. When you can see to the back, it definitely opens things up.
12. Get rid of all clutter and keep only those things you really love.
13. Don't necessarily choose downsized furniture. Sometimes fewer large pieces take up less space than more small ones.
14. Go wild in powder rooms-color expands them better than white.
15. Paint a focal wall

    * Expand your thoughts as well as the space: embrace the fact that your small space is cosy and... perfect!

5 WAYS TO VISUALLY ENLARGE WINDOWS

1. Replace trim around the windows with wider molding or flat craftsman style boards.
2. Attach shutters: either use fixed shutters on either side or wooden duo-fold shutters that appear to be closed on either side and open in the middle.
3. Start window treatments at the ceiling
4. Add to short basement windows by attaching molding to resemble a window frame in front with mirrors in the lower panels. Add a window treatment which extends at least 18" left and right overlapping the "window frame." Prefer not to see the mirrors? Hang a lower valance.
5. Add mirror below to reflect light, then top window and mirror with a stained glass panel.

5 COMMON DECORATING RULES YOU SHOULD BREAK!

Rule 1: Paint ceilings white
Rule 2: Add crown molding
Rule 3: Don't use dark paint in small rooms
Rule 4: Keep houses neutral for resale
Rule 5: Small rooms need small furniture

What we learned:

1,2. White ceilings and crown molding form a line that stop the eye and make ceilings appear shorter. By bringing the paint color up to the ceiling, the eye continues to flow upward. Even the darker black ceiling in the gentlemen's room appears far taller than it did white.
3. Using a dark red in the crossroads room actually made it look larger by giving it presence. The depth of the mural, warmth of the wood floor, and neutral ceiling keep it from seeming too dark.
4. While the neutral rule often holds true, some custom touches such as our dining room floor, painted note in the kitchen, and the stairs, can make a home memorable and make it stand out from the rest. A person who falls in love with a house will pay over market. For example. A house 4 doors from the fauxhouse with the same layout, painted all white with beige carpet, sat on the rental market for 6 months at $1400. The faux house rented in 1 month for $2100.
5. Sometimes a few large pieces work better than a clutter of smaller furniture.

5. UPDATES FOR GREY CONCRETE

1. Paint (gentleman's room, front walk, dining room)
2. Stain (wine cellar)
3. Thin overlays (skimstone-shed, kitchen countertop, downstairs bath and fountain)
4. Modellos® or tape (for "engraved" or inlay look (kitchen entrance, "flagstone" kitchen floor, cellar floor)
5. Stamped-driveways, pathways etc.

6 VISUAL TRICKS FOR SHORT CEILINGS

1. Paint the wall color aprox 6" onto the ceiling and then tape off and paint a faux "tray ceiling" using varied shades of the same color
2. Paint the ceiling the same color as the walls. Even better, use a cloudy fauxed version so that the heavy block of color is softened (this also hides ceiling flaws.)
3. Install up-lighting and avoid overhead lights and ceiling fans.
4. Break up the space into a grid pattern and paint the center of each grid darker
5. Paint the edges a lighter tone and get darker as you move toward the center so the ceiling looks arched
6. A painted sky can make the ceiling appear higher as long as it is broken up visually (A large expanse of blue can appear to be weighing down on you.) Break up the blue with clouds, the gridwork of a trellis, a bird painted in perspective, branches etc. Paint the sky a darker and cooler blue in the center and a lighter and warmer blue near the edges to give the illusion of depth. Clouds should also be painted with greys and a bit of pale pink or yellow to add dimension and depth.

4 STEPS TO MAKING A LARGE ROOM COZY.

1. Use warm colors
2. Divide the area into multiple seating areas
3. Use area rugs to tie together each area and tie in the colors of the room
4. Apply texture to walls such as plaster, grass-cloth, or molding or wood panels

15 UNEXPECTED SOURCES FOR INSPIRATION AND CROSS-OVER PAINTING ITEMS

Look in unusual places for your tools, supplies and inspiration. Go into any store with an eye to what you might be able to use in decorative painting or crafts. These are 10 unusual places we found useful inspiration for Artists4Others:

1. Boat supply warehouse: yielded a scrub brush and extra soft cloth to use with glazes. A key ring with 2 small screwdrivers became indispensable for removing switch-plates and vents.
2. Toy store: Sculptey bakeable clay adds fun texture or can be shaped into grapes, etc to add to a wall finish or cabinet.
3. Sewing store: a rolling tote made for a sewing machine is perfect for transporting heavy paint supplies and colored sewing chalk–wonderful to sketch out murals. Lace, trim, and cording are great for walls.
4. Cross-stitch store: Cross-stitch patterns can be used for real or painted mosaics.
5. Plastics manufacturer: Thin pieces of styrene plastic are not only great for sample boards and mini-trowels for plaster, but can be glued over beadboard, under a chair rail where you want to add removable texture, or painted and glued/stapled over ugly acoustical ceiling tile.
6. Wall paper store: Heavy-duty clay adhesive for hanging murals, fun ideas for wall patterns and colors, papers that can be torn for wall finishes or to peek out under textures, large sponges and plastic smoothers –great for textures.
7. Dollar Store: inexpensive buckets, chip brushes, cheap tablecloths for dropcloths, storage containers, etc
8. Craft store: The non-paint sections often yield great finds–glass beads to glue in the center of a harlequin diamond pattern in a bath; scrap-booking supplies have a wealth of fun items to add to a finish; cake decorating bags and tubes for plasters; plastic grapes to be painted and "rusted" then glued to a wall; cheap pedestals and yard ornaments that can be marbleized or made to look like aged bronze–the possibilities are endless.
9. Restaurant and janitorial supply stores: cheesecloth to be used for glazing or stretched out with plaster troweled through for a snakeskin/elephant-skin texture, tiny takeout sauce containers (great to keep small portions of paint), scrub brushes for glazing, industrial cleaners to clean dried out brushes, paper towels with varied textures for glaze looks or clean-up, bowling-alley wax to be tinted, extra large rolls of plastic wrap to protect toilets, cover paint trays, etc.
10. Office supply store: a laptop or overhead projector for projecting murals, painting software, calculators for measurements, cardboard boxes to organize supplies.
11. Auto supply store: extra-extra fine sandpapers and electric car buffers to burnish and shine lime plasters, decorative tapes that stretch better than other tapes to go around curves in mural work, specialty primers and sealers, Chammie cloth for glazes, and more.
12. Lumber store: Decorative wooden pieces and moldings to update cabinets, create interesting knobs...
13. Fast food restaurants: the Styrofoam container some burgers come in are perfect for pressing thru those pesky switch-plate screws so that you can paint them and keep them from getting lost, or for small pallets for mural paints.
14. Grocery stores: brown grocery bags can be torn and applied to walls, plastic bags can be turned inside out and crumbled to break up brush marks or to wrap around paint trays, wet brushes, and rollers, etc in a glaze finish, wrap Q-tips for tiny clean-up bleed under, pipe cleaners for getting paint out of tiny areas or cleaning sprayers, newspapers for glaze finishes...
15. Gift Shops: tissue paper used for gift bags can be torn for a crumpled paper wall finish, stationary papers used under textures or decoupaged into cabinets, and used in torn-paper finishes. Letter wax and stamps make fun decorative additions to certain wall finishes, painted pots, and accessories.

7 WAYS TO A GREENER, HEALTHIER HOME

1. Use water-based green or very low VOCC paints.
2. Replace old windows with energy-efficient ones.
3. When choosing appliances, choose high-energy ratings
4. Choose low-water-use toilets.
5. Replace synthetic wall-to-wall carpets (which can be toxic, hold dust mites, germs, etc.). Instead, use renewable wood, bamboo, tile or stone and natural fiber area rugs.
6. Don't fill the landfills with old cabinets appliances, etc. Try to paint, plaster over or update without ripping things out. If you do remove cabinets and appliances, donate them to Habitat Restore or a similar organization.
7. The multitude of green products and building methods could fill several books. Study which building materials are toxic (many are), the variety of products, and methods available and make educated choices.

Note: Our landscaper, Chris Jackson, builds cob houses and educated us on green issues at the fauxhouse. We made some mistakes, but did others right and became far more aware.

5 STEPS TO A DRY BASEMENT

1. Check for any signs of mold or mildew. You will need to get rid of either before starting. If you paint over it, mold can come back. Bleach works well on mildew and some mold, however, other mold is resistant to bleach and should be evaluated by an expert.
2. Clean the surface with a bleach solution or TSP so you'll have a clean surface for the paint adherence.
3. Select additives you may want to add to your paint. Anti-mildew additive is available at most paint stores. (Some states require that the store mix in the additive for safety reasons). Paint pouri adds a fresh scent to the wall that will last for weeks.
4. Dryloc® Paint–This product keeps moisture from coming in. We recommend you apply 2 coats. It is sometime difficult to get into the small crevices of cinder block. We found a large scrub brush worked well and quickly in those areas.
5. If you plan to install some version of drywall, sheet plastic can be placed between the 2 layers, or use Great Stuff or other brand blow-in insulation. It is waterproof. But be careful to follow the instructions.

***For added protection, consider a dehumidifier and/or sump pump.

Resources

Learning-Organizations:

Art Leagues
Great source of information and fellowship. Most hold monthly meetings, classes and provide newsletters on upcoming shows, classes and exhibit opportunities. Just do an online search for one in your community. For example, in the DC area there are many: Reston League of Artists, Springfield Art League and others. The largest is: The Art League.

The Art League
Large variety of classes in painting, sculpture and other art forms. Also weekend and travel workshops
105 North Union St.
Alexandria, VA 22314
School: 703-683-2323
www.theartleague.org

International Salon of Artists
The world's top decorative painters meet to share their knowledge and preserve the craft. Certain days/demos open to the public.
www.salonforever.com

Professional Decorative Painters Association (PDPA)
Professional association developing accreditation/certification program.
2132 Market St., Denver, CO 80205
303-893-0330
Info@pdpa.org/www.pdpa.org

Stencil Artisans League, Inc. (SALI)
It's not just for stencilers anymore-- includes stencil, faux and decorative painting. Look for a chapter near you or join one of the online chapters.
National: PO Box 3109
Los Lunas, NM 87031
Salihelp@aol.com
505-865-9119 phone/fax
www.sali.org for local chapter list
Stenciling Roundtable (SRT):
Original online SALI Chapter:
www.stencilingroundtable.org
Atrium on line: Newest SALI online chapter. www.atriumonline.com

Society of Decorative Painters
See website for a chapter near you. Holds monthly meetings and classes. Excellent regional and national painting conferences offering mini-classes by top artists. Membership incl. magazine
316-269-9300
www.decorativepainters.org

Am. Art Pottery Association
www.amartpot.org

Am. Society of Marine Artists
www.americansocietyofmarineartists.com

Craft and Hobby Association
www.craftandhobby.org

Crafts Assoc. of British Columbia
www.cabc.net

Craft Fair List-UK
www.ukcraftfairs.com

The National Concrete Masonry Association (NCMA)
www.ncma.org

National Watercolor Society
www.nws-online.org

National Society of Artists
www.nsartists.org

National Oil & Acrylic Painters Society www.noaps.org

The Painting & Decorators Association, UK
www.paintingdecoratingassociation.co.uk

PDRA (Paint & Decorating Retailers Assoc.) Representation/ certification of the trade, trends, tng DVDs. Publish Faux Finisher.
www.PDRA.org

Portrait Society of America
www.portraitsociety.org

American Society of Portrait Artists
www.ncma.org

Portrait Society of Canada
www.portraitsocietyofcanada.com

Society of Animal Artists
www.societyofanimalartists.com

Society of Gilders
www.societyofgilders.org

Magazines:

American Painting Contractor
free subscription
www.paintmag.com

Artists' E-zine- free by email includes tips, what's new, how-to's, and upcoming charity book and TV opportunities for artists and D-I-Y ers
www.fauxhouse.com

Art Business News-free
jjancsurak@sbcmediaLLC.com

Artistic Stenciler
Free with SALI membership
www.fauxisme.com

Better Homes and Gardens Specialty Publications
www.betterhomesandgardens.com

Chicken Soup for the Artists Soul. Book avail at bookstores or through artists4others. See link at www.fauxhouse.com

Concrete Decor Magazine On-line, (See learning Resource Section) or www.concretedecor.net

Decor Magazine
Trade mag. covers industry news, marketing matters and emerging trends
www.decormagazine.com

Decorative Painter
Full of how to's and ideas. Distributed free to members of SDP.
www.decorativepainters.org

Decorating Solutions
by Harris Publications available at local grocery and bookstores.

E'lan
Articles on Artists in No. VA -celebrating the good life
www.elanmagazine.com

The Gilder's Tip
Published biannually for members of The Society of Gilders
www.societyofgilders.org

Faux Effects World
Includes great projects ideas and recipes using faux effects products. Available at Barnes & Noble.

The Faux Finisher Magazine
Avail. by subscription. Articles about and for Faux Finishers and Decorative Painters.
www.fauxfinishermagazine.com

Fine art magazines are avail. at most large bookstores, art supply stores. Artist4Others has secured deep discounts thru our site for the following magazines: American Artists Magazine, Art and Antiques, Art on Paper, Art News, Artists Magazine, Inked, International Artist,Juxtapox, Painting, Paint Works, The Pastel Journal, Watercolor, Southwest Art, Watercolor Magic. Go to www.fauxhouse.com for discount link.

Paint Magic
by Harris Publications, available at local grocery and bookstores.

PaintPRO
Free digital magazine with information, ideas, calendar of events, training and

a directory of painting schools.
877-935-8906/ www.paintpro.net

Watercolor
An online magazine for watercolor, acrylic artists
www.worldfwatercolor.com

Online Forums:

Artforum
News and critiques of exhibitions in the visual arts, with a contemporary focus. Also online magazine
www.artforum.com

Cennini Forum
Hosted by Studio Products focus is on pictorial painting and painting technique. To help the serious professional and dedicated amateur
www.forums.studioproducts.com

Concrete Countertop Forum
Targeted to countertops.
www.concretecountertops.org

Faux Forum
Sponsored by Patrick Ganino. Open discussion on all faux products & schools. Geared toward decorative painting professionals/enthusiasts to share information, ask questions & post photos. Includes contests, prizes etc
www.fauxforum.com

Fresco Forum
Sponsored by Ilia Anossov. Talk about fresco history techniques and news
www.truefresco.com/dcforum

House of Faux-a site with information geared to decorative painters www.houseoffaux.com.

The Kelly S. King Network of Decorative Finishers Forum
Sponsored by Kelly S. King. Includes how-to's and chats with special areas for specific products primarily: Golden, Adicolor, Perfecto & Modern Masters
www.ksknetwork.com

Muralsplus
Sponsored by MAH since 1997. For faux finishers/muralists, Includes on-line finisher directory, photos, live and archived help, tips, and Faux Effects® product information. (Paid membership required to view full gallery.)
www.muralsplus.com

Plaster Talk
Sponsored by The School of Italian Plasters. Includes discussion about problems, how-to, creative ideas, etc. related to Italian plasters
www.Plastertalk.com

Talk Faux Forum
Includes open discussion on all products & schools. Photo gallery. Free & enhanced membership options. An auction and sales area for individuals buying or selling.
www.talkfaux.com

Wet Canvas
The largest community for visual artists on the Internet/over 100k members. Geared toward canvas and fine art
www.wetcanvas.com

A&E - www.boards.aetv.com
HGTV - www.HGTV.com
DIY Network - www.diynetwork.com
TLC - www.learningchannel.org
This Old House - www.thisoldhouse.com

Conferences:

Art of The Portrait National Conference
Classes and Demos
Quarterly newsletter
www.portraitsociety.com

Concrete Countertop Convention & Trade Show
www.concretecountertopinstitute.com

Fauxcademy of Decorative Finishing
National awards conference for faux and decorative artists. Includes awards and trophies in multiple categories plus learning opportunities: seminars, roundtable discussions, masterminds and demonstrations.
1-800-980-FAUX (3289)
info@kskacademy.com
www.fauxcademy.com

The Faux Event
Annual conference with classes, demos, trade-show and fun!
www.fauxhelp@mbn.com
www.nbm.com/faux

HOOT Annual Conference & Trade Show
Hosted by Heart of Ohio tole painters
614-863-1785
www.heartofohiotole.org

Las Vegas Annual Creative Painting Conv. & Trade Show
Hosted by Jay Sharp. Short & inexpensive classes by top decorative painting instructors. Mostly 3-6 hr projects in watercolor, acrylic & oils.
702-221-8234
www.vegaspaint.com

MAD Penselvania
Short affordable classes in watercolor acrylic & oil. 570-842-0361
www.madpainting.com

Meeting of the Masters
Sponsored by Faux Effects International®
Demonstrations, displays and classes with emphasis on Faux Effects® and Aqua Finishing® solutions line of products 800-270-8871
www.fauxeffects.com

Society of Decorative Painters Annual Convention & Trade Show:
Classes in decorative painting-watercolor, acrylic & oils
316-269-9300
www.decorativepainters.org

National Hardware Show
Paint/Faux represented by PRDA
www.nationalhardwareshow.com

Note: If you know of other learning resources we should include email us thru our website www.fauxhouse.com

Cement/Concrete:

Bella Vernici Architectural Concrete Overlay System Concrete and Stains (as seen on wine cellar floor) distr. by Paintin the Town Faux
www.bellavernici.com
800-549-041
www.paintinthetown.com

D.C. Concrete Technologies
Decorative Concrete Application in the DC area (front walk and kitchen floor)
Justin Velez-Hagan
1-800-283-9498
202-558-6562 fax
Justin@dcconcretetechnologies.com
www.dcconcretetechnologies.com

Exquisite Finishes
by Gary Arvanitopulos-Decorative concrete & faux (as seen in kitchen entrance, countertop and Ode' to Orleans fountain)
814-838-2281/703-831-1383
Gary@exquisite-finishes.com
www.exquisite-finishes.com

Decorative Concrete of Maryland, Inc.
Specializing in Decorative Overlays & Indoor/Outdoor Water Features (as seen on kitchen countertop and side entrance), Dan Mahlmann
301-325-1544
www.decorativeconcreteofmd.com

RS® Crete Concrete Overlay System
by Faux Effects® International
1-800-270-8871
www.fauxeffects.com

Pure Texture
Cement Products donated for
fountain project
517 Medley St.
Greensboro, NC 27406
336-335-3010
336-574-0802 fax
www.puretexture.com

Skimstone
Specialty product troweled over
concrete or used with specialty primer
over floors walls and countertops
Rudd Company, Inc.
1141 NW 50th St.
Seattle, WA 98107
206-789-1000/206-789-1001 fax
Info@skimstone.com
www.skimstone.com

Twig and a Feather, Inc.
Sculpted Walls /Dimensional and
stained concrete overlays in the
Chicago area.
Keren Andra Navarro
1051 East Main, Ste. 102
East Dundee, IL 60118
847-426-2377/847-426-2366 fax
www.twigandafeather.com

Fabric, Canvas and Lace:

Animal and Misc. Lace
Spray paint or trowel sparkling plasters
thru the lace for great cabinet and
wall finishes. (As shown in Chicago
and Small space chapters) see www.
cefaux.com for other examples and
contact us for prices and availability.
info@cefaux.com

Calico Corners-National
Incredible selection of fabrics, lace,
beaded and other trims, tassels etc.
Also custom furniture covering. Stores
are found nationwide.
www.calicocorners.com

Calico Corners - Arlington
Special thanks to the Arlington store
who provided fabric hardware and
custom made roman shades for the
Faux House kitchen.
6400 Williamsburg Blvd.
Arlington, VA 22207
703-536-5488
www.calicocorners.com

Coverups
Drapery Construction and Flower

arranging by Ceil Glembocki
911 Saddleback Ct.
McLean, VA 22102-1317

Discount Fabrics, USA
(and Sabina and Sullivan)
Designer Fabrics at a fraction of the cost:
provided the curtains for Faux House Dining room and bedding fabric for Romantic
Bedroom.
308 Hillswood Ave.
Falls Church, VA
703-241-1555

Luminex USA
U.S distributor of fiber-optic fabrics
12212 Technology Blvd.
Austin, TX 78727
888-219-8020
512-219-5195 fax
info@luminexcorp.com
www.luminexcorp.com

MZ Drapery and Accents
9686 Brittford Dr.
Burke, VA 22015
703-455-3343

Roc-Lon Industries Inc.
Very thin canvas like material, can
be printed or painted for murals or
floor-cloth
1601 Edison Highway
Baltimore, MD 21213
410-522-2505 ext. 1275
www.roc-lon.com

Zuzka for Fabricology Inc.
37 East 18th St., 10th Floor
New York, NY 10003
212-260-1876
212-260-7963 fax
www.zuzka.com
Info@zuzka.com

Faux Schools and Supplies:

Adicolor
A new dimension in finishes-Wide
selection faux products textures and
glazes. See website for US distributors
1 Applewood Cres, Unit 2
Concord, Ontario, Canada
L4K4K11866
www.adicolor.com

**Affiliate Program for Internet
Products Sales**
Sell Your Products on our sites
www.getpaintstuf.com

**Alexandria Paint &
Decorative Center**
Paints, Supplies and a design team
3610 E. King St.

Alexandria, VA 22302
703-379-5800

Antique Mirror Solutions
By AMPS Industries Inc. Complete kits
to distress & antique mirrors. Non-toxic
(as seen on the Faux House hall mirror
doors)
1919 Oxmoor Rd., Ste. 420
Birmingham, AL 35209 USA
205-533-9457
646-415 9368 fax
www.antiquemirrorps.com

Anything But Plain
Faux finishing school teaches faux
finish in all disciplines. Featuring Aqua
Finishing Solutions®
12539 Duncan, Ste. D
Houston, TX 77066
281-444-2070
800-444-1170/281-444-2081 fax
Abp@flash.net/
www.anythingbutplain.com

**Arlington Paint &
Decorative Center**
Sell paint & supplies and have a design
team.
5701 Lee Highway
Arlington, VA 22207
703-534-4477

Artists4Others
Non-profit: Artists using talents for
charities such as Habitat, Hospice and
animal rescue
Adrienne van Dooren
Chair@fauxhouse.com
www.artists4others.com

Art-Stuf
Huge selection of anything to do with
molding supplies. Also airbrushes,
leafing, etc. See online catalog
730 Bryant St.
San Francisco, CA 94107
1-888-ART-STUF
arty@artstuf.com
www.artstuf.com

**Artimatrix Academy of
Architectural Finishes**
Faux classes promoting individual
creativity & expression. Distributor for
Faux Effects© full line of products &

Coral Light
1020 East English St.
Wichita, KS 67211
316-264-2789
Info@artimatrix.com
www.artimatrix.com

Barth's Faux Studio
Las Vegas faux school. Adicolor® Faux
Tool™ Distributor. Barth White, (Living
Room) is the director and primary

instructor. He also does contracting
commissions.
3520 Coleman St.
North Las Vegas, NV 89032
702-631-5959/ 800-998-3289
www.faux.

Beaux-Artes
Decorative grates, hinge straps, door
handle surrounds, moldings, etc.
1012 South Creek View Ct.
Churchton, MD 20733
410-867-0790/410-867-8004 fax
www.beaux-artes.com
Info@beaux-artes.com

BEHR Paints
Sold exclusively at The Home Depot.
1-800-854-0133, ext. 2
www.behr.com

Benjamin Moore Paints
High Quality Paints and expert advice
51 Chestnut Ridge Rd.
Montvale, NJ 07645
Info@benjaminmoore.com
www.benjaminmoore.com

The Business of Creativity
"Left Brain Advice for Right Brain
People" Ketteran Studios
Mt. Airy, MD 21771
301-829-0146
www.thebizofcreativity.com

**Color Wheel Paints
& Coatings**
DC area- paints, supplies and classes
on both faux and concrete finishes
Distributor for Skimstone®, Bella
Vernici®, Modern Masters®, & Oikos® .
Eric Crow
1374 Chain Bridge Rd.
McLean, VA 22101
703-356-8477
www.colorwheel.com

**Coaching: Make your business
rock!**
Individualized training and coaching
program on running and marketing
your faux business.
www.fauxcoach.com

Coral Light
Faux Stone Products Interior/Exterior
lightweight faux stone decorative
pieces, fireplace surrounds and
more. (as seen on master bathtub)
Distributed by Artimatrix
www.artimatrix.com/shop_coral_light.htm

Creative Evolutions
Classes in Decorative Finishing and
online store/Patrick Ganino
16 Main St., Durham, CT 06422
203-421-8423/1-866-775-FAUX
www.creativeevolutions.net
www.fauxwarehouse.com

Daige Pro-Cote Waxer
Wax & applicator for hanging lightweight murals/easily removable
800-645-3323/516-621-1916 fax
info@daige.com/www.daige.com

DecoFinish, LLC
US distributor for Oikos® paints and
plasters. Wide selection of products
and videos available online
2012 NE 155th St.
North Miami Beach, FL 33162
305-940-8022
305-940-8411
www.decofinish.com
Info@decofinish.com

Designer Finishes
Innovative faux finish classes. Wanda
Timmons (kitchen & wine cellar
countertops) is the primary instructor.
Aqua Finishing Solutions® Distributor
266 North State Route 121
Warrensburg, IL 62573
217-672-8822
217-672-3737 fax
www.wandafaux.com
Wandat@wandafaux.com

Donna's Designs
Faux Finish & Business Workshop
private pick 5 classes /Donna Mabrey
Lawrenceville GA 30045
770-985-2285
1-877-884-7935
donna@learnfaux.com
www.learnfaux.com

Dundean Studios
Classes and Products
17 Watchung Ave., Ste. 102
Chatham, NJ 07928
973.635.0505/fax: 973.635.4213
www.dundean.com

**DPAP Decorative Painting
Apprenticeship Program**
On-site restorative painting tng with
top artists.
www.dpap.decoartisans.com

Elephants on the Wall
Paint by number style mural transfers
(such as those seen in the Chicago
kid's room)
2535 N. Altadena Dr.
Altadena, CA 91001
626-794-1415
www.elephantsonthewall.com

Faux Bargains
Good deals on faux and craft supplies
www.fauxbargains.com

Faux Design Studio
Sheri Zeman & Jacek Prowinski
Chicago's Premier School of Decorative Arts. Faux Effects® Distributor.
(Owned by Jacek Prowenski, who did
the Narthex)
101 N. Swift Rd.
Addison, IL 60101
630-627-1011/630-627-1012 fax
fauxdesignstudio@ameritech.net
www.fauxdesignstudio.com

Faux Fingers
Miniature trowels used to get into
corners & small spaces. (Used in Faux
House dining room, wine cellar, and to
create the Venetian plaster mural in the
basement bath.
1713 Woodwind
Austin, TX 78758
412-963-4767
www.fauxfingers.com
sales@fauxfingers.com

Faux Mart
Discounted faux finishing tools and
supplies, wholesale and retail available
online
2830 Holcomb Bridge Rd.
Alpharetta GA 30022
770-641-0884
888-474-0042 toll-free
770-641-3094 fax
www.fauxmart.com
Info@fauxmart.com

Faux Resources
A list of sites and links to everything
faux plus great info
www.fauxresources.com

The Faux Store
Aqua Finishing Solutions® and Faux
Effects® International Professional line
available through
www.fauxstore.com

**Faux Effects® International Fine
Finishing Studio**
3435 Aviation Blvd., Ste. A
Vero Beach, FL 32960
772-778-9044
800-270-8871
772-778-9653 fax
Studio@fauxfx.com
www.fauxeffects.com

Faux Like a Pro
Mark London
119 Braintree St.
Allston, MA 02134
888-765-4950
617-254-8898
617-254-8899 fax
www.fauxlikeapro.com

The Faux Finish School
MAH Decorative Finishes School &
Faux Effects® Distributor
Louisville, KY
1-800-598-FAUX
www.fauxfinish.com

Faux Masters Studio & School
Run by the Hoppe Brothers, well known
for their innovative faux & "stone"
finishes. Faux Effects® Distributor
22855-E Savi Ranch Parkway
Yorba Linda, CA 92887
888-977-3289
Info@fauxmasters.com
www.fauxmasters.com

The Faux School
Both locations provide a variety of
products and tools as well as classes
by Ron Layman (Crossroads to Culture
Room) and top guest instructors

Maryland
Ron Layman, Director
5711 Industry Lane, Ste. 28
Frederick, MD 21704

Florida
663 Harold Ave.
Winter Park, FL 32789
1-877-GET-FAUX
301-668-5100
301-228-3100 fax
Sales@thefauxschool.com
www.thefauxschool.com

Faux Works
School and Faux Effects® Distributor
Barbara Skivington, Director
2638 Willard Dairy Rd., Ste. 106
High Point, NC 27265
336-841-0130
Info@fauxworksstudio.com
www.fauxworksstudio.com

FE Dallas, Inc.
Faux Effects® Distributor/School
Full line of classes
4550 Sunbelt Dr.
Addison, TX 75001
972-733-0028
www.fedallas.com

The Finishing School-NY
School and Faux Effects® Distributor,
faux recipe card series and frequent
buyer points Bob Marx, Executive
Director
50 Carnation Ave., Bldg. #2
Floral Park, NY 11001
516-327-4850
516-327-4853 fax
finschool@aol.com
www.thefinishingschool.com

**The Finishing School -
Pennsylvania**
Faux finish classes by Carol Kemery.
Faux Effects® Distributor
507 North York St.
Mechanicsburg, PA 17055
717-790-3190/717-790-3191 fax
Finschoolpa@aol.com
www.thefinishingschool.com

The Finishing Source- Atlanta
Faux Effects® Distributor. Classes
include faux, furniture, cabinetry, etc.
Caroline Woldenberg, Director
2086 Faulkner Rd.
Atlanta, GA 30324
404-929-9522/404-929-9523 fax
Admin@thefinishingschoolatl.com
www.thefinishingschoolatl.com

Get Paint Stuff
All kinds of faux and craft products and
affiliate program
www.getpaintstuff.com

Heavenly Home Designs
Murals, furniture, decor and ornamentation by Melanie Kershner.
1012 South Creek View Ct.
Churchton, MD 20733
301-855-4244
www.heavenlyhomedesigns.com

Golden Artist Colors, Inc.
Artists colors mediums and textural
acrylics
188 Bell Rd.
New Berlin, NY 13411-9527
800-959-6543/607-847-9228 fax
www.goldenpaints.com

Gotcha Covered
Trompe l'oeil furniture murals and Instruction by Tish Inman
615-230-8689 voice
615-452-5719 fax
igotcha@infionline.ne
www.gotchacovered.com

Jennifer Rebecca Designs
Studio of Decorative Finishes
Jennifer Huehns & Rebecca Klein
Minneapolis/St. Paul, MN
763-792-9244
Studio@jenniferrebeccadesigns.com
www.jenniferrebeccadesigns.com

Karibeth Creations, Inc.
Decorative Painting Studio
and travel teaching
17681 Kenwood Trail
Lakeville, MN 55044
952-898-9155
www.karinbethcreations.com

KB Designs
Faux, residential commercial, concrete
and classes plus website design
serving Deluth and Minneapolis
218-940-3095
www.kbdesigns.com

**Kelly S. King Institute of Deco-
rative Finishes**
Inovative decorative wall and furniture
The Kelly S. King Academy, Inc.
14924 A Circle
Omaha, NE, 68144-5577
1-800-980-FAUX (3289)
info@kskacademy.com
orders@kskacademy.com
800-621-3289 - fax
www.fauxfinishinstitute.com

Ketteran Studios
Murals, classes to include: the seminar
"The Business of Creativity: Left Brain
Advice for Right Brain People"
Mt. Airy, MD 21771
301-829-0146
www.ketteranstudios.com
www.thebizofcreativity.com

Krylon
The nation's leading spray paint
manufacturer, plus exciting specially,
faux & water based paints.
101 Prospect Ave., NW
540 Midland Building
Cleveland, OH 44115
1-8004KRYLON (1-800-457-9566)
www.kylon.com

Len Garon Studios
Fine art and pet portraits
1204 S. Washington St.,#218W
Alexandria, VA 22314
703-300-0211
www.lengaron.com

Liliedahl Fine Art Studio
Liliedahl Video Productions
Classical Oil Painting workshops, DVD
how-to series, and European travel
seminars
Johnnie Liliedahl
808 South Broadway St.
La Porte, TX 77571-5324
281-867-0324/877-867-0324
www.johnnieliliedahl.com
www.lilipubs.com

The Mad Stencilist
Airbrush, stenciling, murals
PO Box 219 / Dept N
Diamond Springs, CA 95619
888-882-6232/530-626-8618 fax
www.madstencilist.com
Questions@madstencilist.com

Murals Your Way
An online resource for purchasing
economical preprinted murals (such as
the Tuscan mural in the Arlington wine
cellar arch)
717 5th St. South
Hopkins, MN 55343
888-295-9764
952-938-4808 fax
www.muralsyourway.com

The Mural School
Murals, figures, marble wood &
portraits & trompe l'oeil classes &
how-to DVDs
Sean Crosby &
Pascal Amblard
168 Elkton Rd., Ste. 209
Newark, DE 19711
302-731-7752
www.themuralschool.com

**Michel Nadaï Advanced School
of Decorative Painting**
Trompe l'oeil, woodgraining & more
"Le Poussou" - 47450 St. Hilaire de
Lusignan - France
Tél.: +33(0)5.53.47.90.24 -
+33(0)6.09.93.09.13
contact@michelnadai.com
www.michelnadai.com

Oikos®
Solvent-free decorative systems/
plasters (as seen in the Arlington 1/2
bath)
Avail in selected paint stores
info@oikos-paint.com
www.oikos-paint.com

Paintin the Town Faux
Distributor: Aqua Finishing Solutions®,
Bella Vernici, Parvati, etc. and 5000 sq.
ft. training facility
Susie Goldenberg, Director
2830 Holcomb Bridge Rd.
Alpharetta, GA 30022
770-641-7641 P
770-641-3094 fax
1-800-549-0414
www.paintinthetown.com
email- info@paintinthetown.com

Parvati Textures Cotton Plaster
Wallcovering System
Distributed by Paintin the Town Faux
2830 Holcomb Bridge Rd.
Alpharetta, GA 30022
770-641-7641
770-641-3094 fax
800-549-0414
www.parvatitextures.com
Info@paintinthetown.com

Patina Studios
Top quality training in everything from
wall glazing to hand painted furniture
and murals.
1620 W. 39th St.
Kansas City, MO 64111
816-561-4103
Learn@patinastudios.com
www.patinastudios.com

Patricia's Palette
Faux Painting and Murals
by Patricia Buzo
651-785-6746
www.Patricias-Palette.com

**Pierre Finkelstein Institute of
Decorative Painting, Inc.**
World renowed for marble & wood-
graining training & specialty brushes.
20 West 20th St., Ste. 1009
New York, NY 10011
888 FAUX ART
212-352-2058 fax
Pfinkel@earthlink.net
www.pfinkelstein.com

**Priscilla Hauser Decorative
Painting Seminars by the Sea**
PO Box 521013
Tulsa, OK 74152-1013
918-743-6072
918-743-5075 fax
PHauser376@aol.com
www.priscillahauser.com

Plaza Artist Materials
Art supplies, DC area
8209 Georgia Ave.
Silver Spring, MD 20910
301-587-5581
customercare@plazaart.com
www.plazaart.com

Prismatic Painting Studios
by Gary Lord, author of several faux
finishing books. Gary's classes include
textures & innovative finishes using his
line of metallic foils (such featured in
the Chicago rectory).
11126 Deerfield Rd.
Cincinnati, OH 45242
513-531-5520/513-931-5545 fax
Info@prismaticpainting.com
www.prismaticpainting.com

Pro Faux
ProFaux product line, tools and full line
of faux classes
1367 Girard St.
Akron, OH 44301
330-773-1983
866-966-3423/636-673-2070 fax
www.profaux.com

Roc-Lon Industries Inc.
Very thin canvas like material, can
be printed or painted for murals or
floor-cloth
1601 Edison Highway
Baltimore, MD 21213
410-522-2505 ext. 1275
www.roc-lon.com

**Sarasota School of
Decorative Arts**
Director, Donna Phelps (as seen in
master bath) Products, classes and
stencils.
5376 Catalyst Ave.
Sarasota, FL 34233
888-454-3289 toll free
941-921-6181/941-921-9494 fax
Info@ssda1.com
www.ssda1.com

Scentco
Scented paint additives, lavender,
vanilla, fresh and more. Lasts months
93 Genesis Parkway
Thomasville, GA 31792
877-723-6826
229-228-6137 fax
www.scentco.net
Info@scentco.net

School of Italian Plasters
Product line, two schools, forum

San Diego:
Doyle and Linda Self
2145b Fern St.
San Diego, CA 92104
619-282-0120/866-336-3393
Doyle@italianplasters.com
www.italianplasters.com

Georgia:
James and Shayna Kirkpatrick
1717 Spring St.
Smyrna, GA 30080
866-560-4444 Toll Free
770-438-0870 Direct Line
770-438-7709 Fax
www.italianplasters.com
James@italianplasters.com

Sherwin-Williams Company
Local store sponsored DC project
Matt Keaney
10880 Main St.
Fairfax, VA 22030
703-591-3770
www.sherwin-williams.com

Sinopia
Finest quality pigments and materials for restoration, interior design and fine arts.
3385 22nd St.
San Francisco, CA 94110
415-824-3180
415-824-3280 fax
pigments@sinopia.com
www.sinopia.com

The School of Applied Arts
Faux finish & painting school, Denver, Colorado- a non-profit, product agnostic top rated school. Free info DVD avail.
1752 Platte St., Ste. 100
Denver, CO 80202
1-866838-8858
info@schoolofappliedarts.com
www.schoolofappliedarts.org

Stencilwerks
School of Decorative Painting
1918 Tilghman St.
Allentown, PA 18104
800-357-4954/610-289-7792 fax
www.stencilwerks.com
Stencilwerks@rcn.com

Terra Bella Finishes
Incredible product line: metalic waxes, pure and peasant paints, textured glaze, sealers,etc.
PO Box 940718
Simi Valley, CA 93094
1-800-771-0602/805-491-2516
www.terrabellafinishes.com

Totum Designs, Inc.
Green faux products and plasters
Contact: Joe Greco
905-951-6574
www.totumdesigns.ca, or
www.learntofaux.com

Tust Studio
Faux and decorative painting classes
PO Box 2245
Pine, AZ 85544
928-476-3344
866-728-1107 fax
www.tuststudio.com
Email laura@tuststudio.com

Vigini Studios
Faux classes, Trompe l'oeil, woodgraining & murals. Also conducts summer Italian Workshop
2531 Boardwalk
San Antonio, TX 78217
210-212-6177
210-212-6183 fax
Info@viginistudios.com
www.viginistudios.com

Wing Enterprises
Little Giant Ladders: Multi-task ladders that configure for stairs, uneven bases, varied height & mini scaffolding
www.littlegiantladders.com

The Wood Icing Company
Textural finishing products that transform furniture, etc (by Rose Wilde as seen in shed cabinet, Arlington)
PO Box 8
Foristell, MO 63348
866-966-3423
636-673-2070 fax
Rosewilde@woodicing.com
www.woodicing.com

Stencils:

To access stencils from multiple sites try:
www.stencilsearch.com

Andreae Designs
Regular & production size stencils projects & full line of supplies
PO Box 300160
Waterford, MI 48330
888-826-3403
www.mystencils.com
Andreaedesigns@hotmail.com

Buckingham Stencils
Stencils, supplies & projection stencils
1710 Morello Rd.
Nanoose Bay B.C. Canada V9P 9B1
888-468-9221
866-468-9227 fax
www.buckinghamstencils.com

Get Paint Stuff
Misc stencils and faux products, many at bargain prices
www.getpaintstuff.com

Jan Dressler Stencils
Mylar and adhesive stencils & great line of tapes for faux grout lines
253 SW 41st St.
Renton, WA 98055-4930
888-656-4515 toll-free
425-656-4515 local
425-656-4381 fax
www.dresslerstencils.com
customerservice@dresslerstencils.com

Heart of the Home Stencils
Stencils incl. popular writing on the wall, tile, garden, eclectic, projects books & videos
1460 Highland Valley Dr.
Chesterfield, MO 63005
636-519-176
888-675-1695 toll-free
208-279-2570
www.stencils4u.com

Lynn Brehm Designs & Natural Accents Stencils
Trompe l'oeil style stencils for walls and murals
6827 Caminito Sueno
Carlsbad, CA 92009
760-744-3986
LSBDesigns@aol.com
www.natural-accents.com

The Mad Stencilist
Fun stencil line to include large animals, windows, etc. Classes incl. airbrush stenciling
PO Box 219 Dept. N
Diamond Springs, CA 95619
888-882-6232 toll-free
530-626-8618 fax
www.madstencilist.com
Questions@madstencilist.com

Modello® Designs
Adhesive stencils and specialty floor and ceiling pattern sets (classes)
2504 Transportation Ave., Ste. H
National City, CA 91950
800-663-3860
800-747-9767
619-477-5607/619-477-0373 fax
Sales@modellodesigns.com
www.modellodesigns.com

Red Lion Stencils
Detailed theorems & stencils for home decor & craft projects
1232 First NH Tpk
Northwood, NH 03261
603-942-8949
603-942-8769 fax
www.redlionstencils.com
Lion@redlionstencils.com

Royal Design Studio
Full stencil line, how-to books DVDs & school (Also see Modello Designs)
2504 Transportation Ave., Ste. H
National City, CA 91950
619-477-3559
800-747-9767
619-477-8193 fax
Sales@RoyalDesignStudio.com
www.royaldesignstudio.com

SayWhat?
Mylar and SayWhat? adhesive lettering stencils, Daige waxer
The Mad Stencilist
Attn: SayWhat?
PO Box 219
Diamond Springs, CA 95619
888-882-6232 toll-free
530-626-8618 fax
SayWhat@madstencilist.com
www.madstencilist.com/saywhat/lettering.htm

Stencil Kingdom
Historically acurate as well as modern selection
28 Greville Rd.
Kenilworth, Warwickshire, CV8 1EL
+44(0) 19260513050
Julie@stencilkingdom.com
www.stencilkingdom.com

Stencil Planet
Full/fun stencil line plus custom adhesive lettering and custom stencil making service
PO Box 90
Berkeley Heights, NJ 07922
877-836-2457 toll-free
908-771-8910 fax
Info@stencilplanet.com
www.stencilplanet.com

Stencilwerks
Stencils from US & England plus specialty torn papers. (classes)
1918 Tilghman St.
Allentown, PA 18104
800-357-4954
610-289-7792 fax
www.stencilwerks.com
Stencilwerks@rcn.com

The Stenciled Garden
Mylar Stencils
6029 N. Palm Ave.
Fresno, CA 93704
559-449-7711
garden@stenciledgarden.com
www.stenciledgarden.com

Vigini Studios
Line of grottesca stencils (classes)
2531 Boardwalk
San Antonio, TX 78217
210-212-6177
210-212-6183 fax
Info@viginistudios.com
www.viginistudios.com
619-477-5607/ 619-477-0373 fax
Sales@modellodesigns.com
www.modellodesigns.com

Services & Supplies-Homes:

Bath and Bath and Idea Center Nolland Plumbing
Full line of plumbing supplies plus support and design help.
6607 Wilson Blvd.
Falls Church, VA 22044
703-241-5000

Floors: Dominion Floors
Experts at instalation repair, and sealing
2433 N. Harison St.
Arlington, VA 22207
703-536-4116
www.dominionfloors.co

Furniture: Curtains, Upholstery and Furniture, LLC
Full line of services and unique furniture collection
6464 Lincolnia Rd.
Alexandria, VA 22312
703-256-2709

Landscaping - Chris Jackson
Landscape design, service, stonework, ponds, waterfalls etc.
703-599-0041
www.rcjacksonlandscaping.com

Nursery - Colesville Nursery
Wide selection of wholesale and retail plants.
804-798-5472/ 804-752-6722 fax
800-856-6773
14011 Nursery Rd.
Ashland, VA 23005
www.colesvillenursery.com

Picture Framing: Hanging Treasures
hangingtreasurers@yahoo.com

Remodeling/Custom Homes:
Action Home Construction, Inc.
Joe Meager
4909 Lincoln Ave.
Alexandra, VA 22312
703-914-5655

Rugs:
Oriental Rugs and More
Beautiful Selection to incl. Sphinx carpets as seen in Gentlemen's Room and great prices Corner Premium Outlets Leesburg, VA (Washington DC area)
703-779-2990
241 Fort Evans Rd. NE
Leesburg VA 20176
www. premiumoutlets.com

Windows:
Thompson Creek Windows
Custom manufacturing of windows and replacement windows (serving Maryland, Washington DC and Northern Virginia.)
8805 Annapolis Rd.
Lanham, MD
866-57-CREEK
www.thompsoncreek.com

Services Misc.:

Catering:
Anne-Marie Schmidt
Star Catering
2000 Mt. Vernon Ave.
Alexandria, VA 22310
703-549-8090
www.starcateringevents.com

Flowers: Westover Florist
Westover Shopping Center,
Arlington, VA
1-800-517-0882
service@blossomflorists.com
www.blossomflorists.com

Pet preservation - Keep My Pet
Preserves your choices and your pet. Special process for pets (not taxidermy) Mail service from across the USA
www.keepmypet.com
571-239-6656

Services Marketing:

Coaching for Faux Business
Faux Coach helps you explode your growth and profits
www.fauxcoach.com

Communications Creativity Publication Support
by Marylyn Ross
209 Church St., PO Box 909
Beuna Vista 81211/719-395-8659
ann@communicationcreativity.com

Media Connections-
Media Services/PR Firm
269-873-3373
Michele Sobota
mediaconnections@sbcglobal.net

Red Hot Copy
Copywriting seminars and Home Instruction source
www.redhotcopy.com

Steven List
Motivational Speaker and management consulting
512-246-3533
www.stevenlist.com

Graphic Production
by Vicky Nuttall
443-2531868
www.shredvicky.com

Vendely Communications, Inc.
Public relations and marketing services
4609 Ventura Canyon Ave.
Sherman Oaks, CA 91423
818-783-3707

Website Design
by Valerie Burchett
Has an artist's special for basic website
5436 Butterfield Dr.
Colorado Springs, CO 80918
Burchett@gmail.com

The House that Faux Built

Transform Your Home with Paint, Plaster, and Creativity

Can't find this book at your local bookstore?

4 easy ways to Order:

- ON-LINE: www.fauxhouse.com
- PHONE: 1-800-345-6665
- FAX: (603) 357-2073
- MAIL: Copy or mail original form to:
  Pathway Book Service
  P.O. Box 89
  4 Whitebrook Road
  Gilsum NH 03448

Quantity Discounts:

Call about quantity discounts for as few as 10 books, larger case discounts, or individualized print runs or personalized dust jackets for your corporation or school.

Ideal For:
- ➻ Gifts
- ➻ Fund-raisers
- ➻ Real Estate Professionals
- ➻ Architectural and Design Firms
- ➻ Art Schools and Universities
- ➻ Promotions
- ➻ Book Clubs

Check out the new "how to" series of DVDs available at www.fauxhouse.com

---

THE HOUSE THAT FAUX BUILT
Amazing Transformations and Inspirational Ideas for your Home

Order Form

Check your local bookstore or order here:

Name: _____

Address: _____

City: _____

State: _____ Zip _____

Phone: _____

Email Address: _____

Book Quantity: _____ Book(s) x $38 each = $_____ total
(Shipping and sales tax are included in our price)

_____ Check made out to Pathway Book Service (enclosed) or

_____ Charge my: ____ VISA ____ Mastercard ____ Discover

Card Number _____

Exp. Date _____/ _____ Code: _____

MAIL ORDERS:
Pathway Book Service
P.O. Box 89
4 White Brook Road
Gilsum NH 03448
WEB: www.FauxHouse.com
PHONE ORDERS: 1-800-345-6665
FAX ORDERS: (603)357-2073

*** Quantity Discounts are available for 10 or more books, cases and wholesale. Large print runs can be personalized with your school or company logo, information, or specialty chapters.